College AND Retirement – You CAN Do Both!

Strategies for Success in Today's Economy - Second Edition

Scott T. Moffitt

Best Wishes

College AND Retirement – You CAN Do Both!

Copyright 2013 by Scott T. Moffitt

Loveland, Ohio 45140

ISBN 978-0-9634412-2-5

Printed and bound in The United States of America

Fidlar Doubleday, Inc.

College AND Retirement - You CAN Do Both!

Second Edition

Scott T. Moffitt

College AND Retirement - You CAN Do Both!
Second Edition

Table of Contents

Dedication

This book is dedicated to my wife Cindy and our four beautiful children: Mary Grace, Alexander Thomas, Andrew Lawson, and Anna Marie, whose unconditional love and support have provided me the desire and inspiration for taking on this project.

Acknowledgements

In the pursuit of completing this second edition it became very clear to me that this was a project that I would simply not be able to do on my own. A blessed life that keeps me running from meetings to speaking engagements, to kids events and the many other things I find myself involved with allows very little time to singularly take on such a monumental task as writing a book.

If not for the family, friends, staff and colleagues that I am so blessed to have in my life this book would be only a dream. Not only were these wonderful people supportive in my pursuit of this project, they rolled up their sleeves and spent countless hours writing, editing and discussing the book with me: truly a collaborative process.

Others were simply understanding about my time and schedule and allowed me the flexibility to work on the book as needed. Many of these people are probably not even aware of how they were helpful, however I am and I am very appreciative.

   To all of you, I simply and sincerely say thank you.

Scott T. Moffitt

About the Author

Scott Moffitt is the co-founder, President and CEO of the Summit Financial Group, Inc. based in Loveland, Ohio. His firm, since its inception in 1996, has been rooted in providing community-based financial education, thus helping individuals and families to make wise decisions regarding their immediate financial needs and long-term dreams.

Scott is the co-founder of College Planning Relief®, the nation's best educational system for late-stage college planning. Mr. Moffitt is one of the leading financial professionals in this area and as such, his expertise in college planning is regularly sought by other financial planners across the country. Scott and his staff regularly train and teach financial professionals on the aspects of college planning.

Scott has consistently been recognized and awarded on both local and national levels for his expertise in financial and college planning. Over the last decade, he has spoken to thousands of people nationwide about various financial topics. His first book, *"College and Retirement, You CAN Do Both"*, was published in 2010.

A native of Cincinnati, Scott and his family reside in the Morrow area. He and his wife Cindy have been married since 1995 and have four children: Mary Grace, Alexander, Andrew and Anna. Scott and Cindy are very active in the local youth sports organizations and attend Montgomery Community Church.

Introduction

I have been working in the field of college planning for over a decade. My attention to this area grew out of the critical need to provide my clients with solid ways to meet their short and long-term monetary goals. I have spoken to thousands of families in my college planning seminars and I am pleased to say I have the ideas, concepts and knowledge to develop an individual plan for parents so they can afford college without sacrificing their own retirement!

This book is intended to help the families of college bound high school students develop a comprehensive plan that allows them to maintain their lifestyle today, pay for college tomorrow, and plan for a successful retirement in the not so distant future. Short-term college planning is a relatively new discipline for financial advisors and I have become an expert in orchestrating individual plans for such families. Over the last two decades the cost of college has increased three times greater than the normal rate of inflation. During the same time period, an increased number of high school graduates continued their formal education. Add to this an economy that has seen its share of ups and downs, and the financial pressures on parents of soon-to-be college freshmen have escalated beyond imagination. Short-term planning for paying for college is now an essential component in family finances. I will guide you through the appropriate processes to develop the best plan for your family.

It is quite common for a family with multiple college bound children to spend on higher education an amount equal to or greater than the value of their home. The real shock comes when they realize this will take place over only a few short years!

This does not have to be the case. I will show you numerous ways to avoid thousands of dollars of unnecessary expense when paying for college. I will also show you how to navigate through the college years without jeopardizing your own financial future.

Maintaining a usual and comfortable standard of living today while paying for college is certainly daunting to parents. College that was once many years away is now staring them in the face. So is the realization that they are quickly approaching the halfway point in their working careers with less money saved towards college and retirement than they intended to have by now. I will guide you through a process that helps you to determine what you can realistically afford to pay for the college education of your children.

Life has been good for us compared to prior generations. We have seen an increased standard of living and a quality of life that our parents and grandparents would never have conceived. It has all come with a price however.

Since the 1940's there has been a steady decrease in the annual savings rate of American families while the number of two-family incomes has increased dramatically. So even though we are living bigger and better, it is costing us more to do so, and often has come at the cost of saving for our future: college and retirement specifically. I can help you to protect your retirement savings while developing a plan to pay for college.

Parents are very conscious of the fact that the pressure is definitely on them to plan for some huge expenses in a short period of time. Then they realize their teenagers will soon be young adults and must be a part of this planning process.

Talking to teens is not the easiest task for most parents, but you must remember that this does involve "their" future and "your" money! I will provide you with some discussion points to talk about and to explore with your teens concerning career and college selections. You probably already realize the choices made will weigh heavily on the design of your "paying for college" plan.

The book will discuss the impact of 529 Plans as well as Minor Accounts on financial aid, but because those are long-term investment accounts that offer little or no benefit to families with students who are in high school, I will not discuss the advantages or disadvantages of contributing to those plans.

There will be several strategies in the chapters that may seem counter-intuitive to long-term planning. Many will likely raise the eyebrows of uninformed financial advisors or CPAs. As you read through the material, review the case studies and begin to develop your own plan, remember that you are preparing to spend, quite possibly, hundreds of thousands of dollars inside of only a handful of years... so keep an open mind.

This book will get you well on your way to the three big E's in financial planning for college: educate, evaluate, and execute. Educate yourself about financial aid; evaluate where you are financially and where you want to be after your children's college years; then execute a logical and realistic plan for your immediate, short-term and long-term money goals. This will go a very long way to clear a path to your successful financial future while at the same time, lower total costs, reduce your stress, and navigate the often overlooked rapids.

Scott T. Moffitt

1

Educate, Evaluate, & Execute

Why bother? This is a question I am asked often about this process. Then I hear, "It seems so complicated!" It is not really complicated and we must bother to follow the three E's because in my review of countless family experiences with paying for college, without any real plans in place, it became all too apparent that their actions were based on erroneous assumptions about financial aid. Those mistakes were recognized <u>after</u> the family unnecessarily spent thousands of dollars and missed multiple opportunities for cost savings.

I'll explain why career and college selection is critical in the paying for college plan so that you do not end up realizing after the fact, that changing majors and/or colleges expands the number of school years with a considerable increase in the total cost of college while delaying income from work.

I want you to avoid getting your own degree from the *School of Hard Knocks*. That is the "school" where so many Moms and Dads have learned the hard way about college financial aid and regretted it! That means dispelling bad assumptions while developing a plan as you work to educate yourself on financing college, evaluating your options, and executing the roadmap to success.

Reading this book is the beginning of your **Education** process. I have filled the chapters with excellent tips as well as obstacles and traps to avoid. If you follow the strategies that I teach you here, you and your college bound son or daughter will be far more likely to make educated and informed decisions about the college process.

Once you are informed and have a general understanding of the college and financial aid landscape it is time to **Evaluate** how your family fits into the system. The first two steps in the evaluation process are to determine your family category for aid and your initial **Expected Family Contribution** (**EFC**).

The evaluation stage must also include a couple of key financial analyses; **cash flow** and **retirement**. Analyzing cash flow is important to determine how much of your income can be used to pay for college and/or to service debt on the college loans. The retirement projection will allow you to determine how much, if any, of your assets you can pledge to college without jeopardizing your retirement. There will be much more on this later.

It is during this stage in the process that we also identify and prioritize other financial goals that may impede or impact the amount of money that Mom and Dad are able to contribute to college. Are you planning to start a business, purchase a vacation home or make a career change that will reduce your income? These factors must be considered before you determine how much you can commit to college.

At this point and only after the Educational and Evaluation processes have been completed are you able to develop and **Execute** a successful college plan. Your paying for college plan should include career profiling, a detailed college selection process, identification of annual cash flow resources, loan evaluation and finally a comparison of what each college is actually offering in financial support.

2

What is "Financial Aid?"

Financial aid provides access to money or resources offered by federal and state governments as well as colleges to help students pay for the cost of a college education. Aid does not necessarily mean "free money." There are numerous types of aid available including educational loans that are paid back over time, work study that is earned along the way and academic and athletic scholarships that are not repaid but require ongoing minimum academic levels of performance.

Grants and scholarships are considered **gift aid** and do not have to be repaid. They are usually based on **merit** (grades, class rank, college entrance testing etc.) or **financial need**. Some scholarships are renewable and may have minimum GPA requirements. College work study programs and educational loans are called **self-help aid** and are usually based on **financial need**.

The federal, state and college need-based financial aid systems are government supported programs. In order to receive financial assistance, the family and/or student must show **financial need.** This need is determined by completing the **Free Application for Federal Student Aid (FAFSA)** which is used by every accredited college and university in the United States to evaluate the eligibility of any student who applies for financial aid.

The **FAFSA** is not new. In fact the federal formula I will discuss later was adopted by Congress as part of the Higher Education Act of 1986. **FAFSA** and the financial aid process have received much attention in recent years as the cost of a college education has increased dramatically, leaving families faced with the challenge of finding ways to afford to send their children to college.

The information provided on the **FAFSA** is analyzed using the **Federal Methodology (FM)** formula. This formula mathematically calculates the **Expected**

Family Contribution (EFC) which is the amount the family is expected to contribute annually towards the student's college education.

The **EFC** is based on many factors including, but not limited to, income and assets of both parents and student as well as the number of children in the family in college. Ultimately, the EFC will be used to determine the student's eligibility to receive financial aid for the balance of the cost.

Every year, high schools, communities and school districts normally conduct what are referred to as "**Financial Aid Nights**." The meetings are typically intended to show parents and students how to complete the federal aid form (**FAFSA**) and to tell families what type of financial aid is available. These evening meetings are usually quite informative.

A few hundred select private universities require applicants to complete the **Profile Form (PF)** in addition to the FAFSA. This form requires registering with The College Board prior to submission. The **PF** uses the **Institutional Methodology** (**IM**), a formula similar to the **FM**, but requires greater detail of a family's finances. Many private schools and a few state schools will use this alternative formula (**IM**) to disburse the funds they directly control.

The collegiate resources called **endowments** are typically the most overlooked source of financial aid money. Private schools in particular tend to have more endowment money earmarked for tuition assistance than public colleges. That is one reason you need to compare all colleges that will provide the desired education outcome because a particular private school could cost less overall than a public institution depending upon the amount of aid offered as well as other variables. I will explain more on those comparisons later.

The financial aid package awarded is predominately based on the initial or base year application. Annual resubmission of the **FAFSA** is required, however the award package typically does not change much from the first year. There are some key exceptions to this: radical change in income or assets for the family in either direction; change in the number of children in college; and a change in a high school student's grades all can impact the aid package. I will share some examples in subsequent chapters.

3

Determining Financial Need

The financial aid system presumes that most families are able to contribute some money toward educational expenses. How much the family is expected to pay is determined by formulas using the information you provide on the **Free Application for Federal Student Aid (FAFSA)** and in some cases on the **Profile Form**. The <u>difference</u> between the amount the family is expected to contribute annually (**Expected Family Contribution** or **EFC**) and the <u>total</u> **Cost of Attendance (COA)**, represents the student's **Financial Need (FN)**.

In addition to the **Federal Methodology (FM)**, a few select private colleges use what is referred to as

Institutional Methodology (**IM**) to calculate the **Financial Need** and **EFC**. Private colleges and some public schools have their own aid to award from their endowment funds so they typically ask for more information than what is available on the **FAFSA**. Those schools use the **Profile Form** or their own financial aid form to collect additional financial details and they may also ask for copies of your tax records, especially if you own a business.

Financial Need (**FN**) is the <u>maximum</u> amount of aid that a family may receive, however it is <u>not guaranteed</u>. The process to determine a student's Financial Need is called **Needs Analysis**. The amount of aid received cannot exceed the total **Cost of Attendance** (**COA**) of the educational institution. Need is calculated using the following formula which classifies a family into one of three categories:

Cost of Attendance (COA)	**$35,000**
– **<u>Expected Family Contribution (EFC)</u>**	**- <u>15,000</u>**
= **Financial Need (FN)**	**= $20,000**

Category One families may receive <u>most</u> of school costs covered via financial aid if they apply for it properly. This is predicated on the family choosing a school that is willing to cover a high percentage of the family's need. **Category Two** families may receive <u>some</u> financial aid however their challenge is how to maximize aid through proper college selection and figure out how to pay for the balance. **Category Three** families will not likely qualify for any need-based financial aid. Their challenge is how to pay for school, so looking at tax strategies may be beneficial for them. Every family should determine its category and estimate its **Expected Family Contribution** (**EFC**) before beginning the school selection process.

Tuition, fees, room and board are often the only "costs" parents initially consider when it comes to the **Cost of Attendance** (**COA**) but for determining **Financial Need** (**FN**) the colleges and universities also consider books and supplies, personal expenses, transportation on campus, round-trip travel to and from home during school vacation periods, childcare, personal computers and many other factors.

The school can also consider extenuating circumstances for families with high medical expenses, disability, death in the family or recent job layoff or loss, or any other circumstance that may adversely impact the family's ability to pay for schooling. Since this information cannot be communicated on the financial aid forms, it is important for the student to bring these issues to the attention of the university **Financial Aid Officer** (**FAO**).

Some institutions will meet 100% of the student's total financial need while others will meet a significantly smaller amount. The difference between what the school will pay and the **COA** is the **Gap**.

Once we know the **COA**, the **EFC** and the **percent of need** met by the institution, we will be able to determine with reasonable accuracy the family's annual out of pocket expenses as shown in this illustration:

(COA - EFC) = FN	**$20,000**
x **% of FN** not met by College	x **60%**
= GAP	**$12,000**
EFC	**$15,000**
+ Gap	**+12,000**
= Annual Out of Pocket Expense for the Family	**$27,000**

Many families are taken aback by their **EFC**. Some families are then surprised to see that the school will not meet all of their financial needs. So, before applying to colleges it is essential to evaluate each school based on its potential ability to meet your total financial need. If a **GAP** is present, plans must be made to handle the additional expense.

Determining Financial Need

Student's and Parents' Contributions – Income and Assets

A family is required to first complete the FAFSA in January of the student's senior year in high school. Both parents and student will need to report all income using tax data from the preceding year (last half of junior year and first half of senior year in high school), defined as the "base year." Since income data reported on the FAFSA comes from your federal tax data it can be beneficial to utilize planning strategies that minimize your income in your "base" year.

Parents' and student's contributions (income and assets) are not viewed equally in the calculations. Student's assets and income are deemed more available than are those of the parents and are thus assessed more heavily in the financial aid formulas.

Your **Adjusted Gross Income (AGI)** from IRS Forms 1040, 1040A or 1040EZ as well as the **AGI** of your student are reported on the **FAFSA**. The **FAFSA** is different from your tax return in that it requires you to add back income items that are not taxable to you on your tax return. For example, retirement contributions and tax exempt interest income are added back in to your income on the **FAFSA**.

It is possible that assets that are increasing your **EFC** may be able to be moved into other investment vehicles that do not count against you in the financial aid process. Before moving or re-titling any assets, you need to make sure it will be helpful. Tax consequences and risks of the new investment must be considered.

Generally a student's limited income will only have a minor impact and the benefits he/she receives from working (being in the working world, on the job experiences, learning responsibility, working with others who are not friends, etc.) can far outweigh the reduction in aid resulting from the income.

<u>Aid or Tax Planning?</u>
If your family falls into **Category One** or **Two** your best option is to make sure you have structured your assets in such a way as to maximize the aid that you may receive. A family usually ends up in **Category Three** due to substantial income and/or assets that are difficult if not impossible to shelter from the aid calculations, however there may be some tax reduction strategies incorporated in the paying for college process. Using strategies to move income or assets to the student who is in a lower tax bracket may be wise.

Summary

In this chapter you have learned that what you are expected to pay for college is called the Expected Family Contribution (**EFC**) and it is determined through either the Federal Methodology (**FM**) or the Institutional Methodology (**IM**) depending on whether the colleges are public or private. The information used to determine **EFC** and the **FN** is reported by you on the Free Application for Federal Student Aid (**FAFSA**) and in some cases on the **Profile Form**.

The total cost of attendance (**COA**) involves much more than tuition, room, and board. Financial need (**FN**) is the difference between what college costs (**COA**) and what you are expected to pay (**EFC**). Sometimes a **Gap** exists requiring additional out of pocket expenses for the family. Your earnings and assets, as well as those of your student, impact the formulas (**FM** and **IM**) considerably, so advance financial planning is essential to maximize the aid that may be available for college.

A closer look at the Free Application for Federal Student Aid (**FAFSA**) is now in order.

4

FAFSA & False Assumptions

The Free Application for Federal Student Aid
(**FAFSA**) was created over two decades ago as a
result of the Higher Education Act of 1986 by the US
Congress. It has had some revisions since then, but
essentially it has changed very little. Completion of
this form is the ONLY option available to families
who seek federal financial aid for college. Every
accredited college and university in the United State
requires the **FAFSA** to evaluate the eligibility of
students who apply for financial aid. Learning about
the **FAFSA** is another important step in being
educated about financial aid.

A family may submit the **FAFSA** as early as January
1 of the student's senior year. As the name implies,
there is no cost to file the form which can be

completed electronically or in paper form and mailed. Annually, approximately 70% of the applications have errors or omissions that result in lost available potential aid. Schools are required to audit 30% of the applications, meaning they seek additional documents from families to substantiate submitted information.

You have three options to complete the FAFSA. The recommended option is to complete it on-line at www.FAFSA.ed.gov. Or, you may download a PDF of the application from www.FAFSA.ed.gov/options.htm. Last, you may complete a paper application that can be requested by calling 1-800-4-FED-AID.

When you complete the FAFSA you will need the following records available to you:

- Social Security numbers – Parents & Students
- W2 Forms & other records of money earned for the prior year
- Tax returns from prior year
- Child Support records
- Current records for stocks and bonds
- Current bank statements
- Current business & farm records

If you have not yet completed your prior year's tax returns, you should calculate your Adjusted Gross Income and taxes paid according to applicable IRS instructions.

The single most frequent mistake (and) subsequently the most costly one) is the failure to submit the form based on an assumption that a family will not qualify for any aid. Far too often parents make this erroneous assumption based exclusively on their income and they do not even bother to complete the form. Parent income is only one of **seven** factors that are taken into account to determine a family's financial aid eligibility. It is not unheard of for families with six figure incomes to still qualify for financial aid.

Another false assumption is that having money in non-retirement accounts seriously hurts one's chances of obtaining financial aid. The fact is that the closer you are to retirement age the more money you are allowed to have in non-retirement accounts that will not count against you in the financial aid calculations.

Families with lower incomes also think they will automatically qualify for financial aid and fail to do other planning. Again, those **seven** factors apply to all families and will have negative or positive influences on the amount of financial aid a student might be eligible to receive. Planning ahead and submission of the **FAFSA** are both important.

You may not like the old saying, "first come, first served," but a portion of federal aid that is distributed is done so on that basis. Waiting until you have all of your income and financial data together and your income taxes completed prior to submitting the **FAFSA** may cause you to miss out on monies for which your family qualifies. It is not only accepted, but expected, that you will submit the **FAFSA** with estimates of your financial data from the previous year.

About a week after submitting your **FAFSA**, you will receive a **Student Aid Report (SAR)** which tells you your **EFC.**   At any time after you receive this report, you can "update" your **FAFSA** by replacing your original estimates with actual numbers from your tax return.

You should make every effort to complete and submit the **FAFSA** in the month of January, and update it at your earliest opportunity.

Now that you know it is important to submit FAFSA and to do it in a timely manner, I need to address errors that could get the application returned to you and cause a four to six week delay in processing which is as costly as turning the form in too late.

If you are divorced and sharing custody of your college bound student, then determining whose parental income and assets to use on the form is crucial, especially if there are step-parents involved. The household in which your child spends the majority of his/her time is the household income and assets that should be used.

By household I mean just that: the income and assets of the step-parent in that house, regardless of his/her financial involvement in supporting the soon-to-be college student, are included on the **FAFSA**. An exception to this would be a non-married adult living in the home. That person's assets and income are not to be included. The parent who the student is not living with the majority of the time may also be asked to complete a supplemental form.

Calculating, even estimating, your household income improperly can also cause issues for you. Many people wrongfully assume household income means simply transferring their adjusted gross income (**AGI**) from the federal tax forms, but they fail to realize that contributions to a pre-tax retirement plan (IRA, 401k, 403b or 457 plan) must be added to that **AGI** to get the household income on the **FAFSA.** That oversight means under-statement of income.

5

Differences in Federal & Institutional Methodologies

A basic understanding of the two methods to determine the amount of Expected Family Contribution (**EFC**) is important, especially if public and private colleges are being considered. There are some similarities and significant differences in what these sets of formulas count or do not count when computing your **EFC**.

I have established that public aid involves the Federal Methodology (**FM**) and private aid involves Institutional Methodology (**IM**). Many public schools require forms in addition to **FAFSA** and some private schools require the **FAFSA** and a **Profile Form** which collects more detailed financial data on the family. Many states also use the **FAFSA** to award their state aid. For a list of schools that use the **IM Profile** form you may go to the web site https://profileonline.collegeboard.com/index.jsp .

You have learned that the income and assets of parents (and step-parents) and students are included in both methods to judge your ability to pay for college. Both **FM** and **IM** make allowances to protect income and assets. Other factors include the ages of parents or independent students, the number of students in the family attending college at the same time, and the number of family members.

The equity in your home/primary residence is excluded in the **FM** computations for the vast majority of state schools. Not so for the **IM** where the home value is included but often capped at a percentage of the family's income level. Since the private schools are spending their own institutional funds they want a larger contribution from families with high home equity. This is one of those questions to ask the college **FAO** so you will know how your home is considered. Note that any other real estate owned, such as vacation and rental properties will be counted in your assets for **FM** and **IM**.

FM does not count "family farms" if the family lives on the farm and materially participates in its operation. Neither the farm house nor the farm business is counted. Under the **IM**, the value of any farm property is considered an asset. **FM** also does not count the value of a family owned and controlled small business (with 100 or fewer fulltime equivalent employees) but **IM** does count it.

IM usually looks into the finances of non-custodial parents and requires a minimum contribution from students toward the **COA**. **IM** also gives more special allowances for savings for each pre-college child, an emergency reserve account, and higher assessment of the income of independent students. Remember too that **Financial Aid Officers (FAO)** at the colleges also have the autonomy to exercise professional judgment when aware of special circumstances.

IM requires a minimum contribution from students. **FM** does not count assets when the family makes below a certain income threshold and does not expect a family contribution towards the **COA** for low **AGI**.

Other factors that may make the **IM** different are a provision for a set-aside fund for younger siblings' educational costs, addition of some losses on the 1040 tax form, and some options of making allowances for pre-college tuition paid for the student's siblings.

One final difference involves due dates of the forms. You should be ready to file the **FAFSA** every year as of January 1 beginning the senior year even though it is accepted up to 18 months later. Many colleges that use the **IM** have submission dates prior to January 1 of the senior year. Filing the forms as soon as possible after the submission period is open is an excellent idea to assure that financial aid resources are available.

Make careful note of the form(s) and due date(s) for each school being considered. I recommend you create a chart with the colleges and due dates of all forms because colleges have zero tolerance for late filing.

6

Gift Aid & Federal Work Study Programs

Students who work in the **Federal Work Study (FWS)** program to help offset some of the college costs, work on or off campus at minimum wage or slightly higher. The important added benefit is that the student's wages in **FWS** are exempt from the aid formulas when other wages earned by the student are assessed at a rate up to 50 cents on the dollar. This is campus-based aid and the work must relate to the student's field of study and the maximum hours/earnings are capped at the amount of the awarded aid.

In recent years more schools and the general public have used the words *grant* and *scholarship* to mean essentially the same. Some scholarships are awarded based on need. However, traditionally they are based on merit in the arts, athletics, or academia. Some colleges now give scholarships based on a combination of merit and need. It makes a difference to you whether or not the scholarship is used to meet need or to reduce your **EFC** since the latter lowers what the federal government and school expects you to pay.

You want to reduce the EFC because it represents your <u>minimum</u> out of pocket expense. For example, a school with a **COA** of $30,000 and a family with an **EFC** of $20,000 has a **need** of $10,000. They know the university will meet 50% of the **need** so they have a **Gap** of $5,000. If they receive a $5,000 scholarship and it is applied to their **EFC** they now have to pay $15,000 ($20,000 less $5,000). With the **EFC** at $15,000 the **need** goes to $15,000 and the college will meet 50% of the need for the family or $7,500.

This family then has to come up with their EFC of $15,000 plus find a way to pay for the Gap of $7,500 created when the university only met 50% of their need. The family has to pay $15,000 EFC plus find $7,500 in loans for a total of $22,500. The minimum out of pocket for the family is $15,000.

If that $5,000 goes to the **need** and not to the $20,000 **EFC** of the family, the $10,000 **need** is reduced to $5,000 and the college pays $2,500 (50%) of that need. The unmet need or **Gap** is then $2,500. While the family still needs to come up with a total of $22,500, the minimum out of pocket for the family is $20,000.

Grants and scholarships come in several different forms. Colleges award them from the private funds available to them from a variety of sources including endowment funds or scholarships named after a donor or in honor of another person. They can be based on merit and/or need and become part of the student's aid package. Often, scholarships are established by donors and then offered to students who need aid and are enrolling in a special field at a college.

It is interesting to note that grants from a college's private resources are not taxpayer money so the only rules regarding their use are established by the schools that control them. There is no limit on the size of private college grants but it is obvious that the wealthier colleges have more money to award than the less financially secure ones.

There are also grants available from the state of residence and in some cases from other states if a reciprocal agreement exists between the states. These grants are based on need and the amount of tuition the college charges.

Some federally sponsored grants may award individual students up to four or five thousand dollars for one or more years. The federal **Pell Grant** is based on need ($5,550 at the time of this publication – see www2.ed.gov/programs/fpg) and is awarded only to US citizens or eligible non-citizens. Everyone who fills out the **FAFSA** automatically qualifies for a Pell Grant. The actual award is determined by the federal government and is based on need.

The federal **Academic Competitiveness Grant** (**ACG**) (up to $750 the first year and $1,300 the second year) is based on high school academic performance while the **National Science and Mathematics Access to Retrain Talent Grant** (**National SMART Grant**) (up to $4,000 a year) is available to third and fourth year students in degree programs in certain "high need" fields as defined by the US Department of Education.

The **Teacher Education Assistance for College and Higher Education Grant** (**TEACH**) (up to $4,000 a year) is available to college students who plan to teach in schools serving low-income families and who attend colleges which have elected to participate in the program. A four-year teaching commitment is required after graduation and failure to comply within eight years turns the grant into a repayable, unsubsidized Stafford Loan.

While the colleges have no say over the **Pell**, the **ACG** and the **National SMART Grant**, the institutions administer the **Federal Supplemental Educational Opportunity Grant (SEOG)**. The colleges may disburse the grant money in awards from a hundred dollars up to several thousand dollars.

The vast majority of scholarship money comes from the colleges themselves, but there are also "outside" scholarships that come from organizations not associated with the colleges. These scholarships may be provided by the local teachers' association, a foundation, the parent teacher organization, a local business, the chamber of commerce, a religious group or a parent's employer. Such scholarships are usually based on merit more than need.

I have just reviewed the most common federal assistance programs. There are several other possible opportunities from a variety of federal departments including:

- Department of Veterans' Affairs
- Disabled American Veterans
- The United States Army
- AmeriCorps
- Department of Health & Human Service

- Department of Labor

A little known fact is that scholarships/grants not associated with the college may end up benefiting the institution rather than the student if the **EFC** and awarded aid for need exceed the **COA**. In that case, the college may reduce its financial aid award by as much as the outside scholarship by taking funds back from the loan or grant. Obviously it would be best to have the loan reduced and not lose the grant money since it does not have to be paid back. In some cases you may be able to convince the **FAO** of the college to let you use some of the outside college scholarship to reduce the **EFC**.

Athletic scholarships are merit aid and tend to garner more news coverage than **academic merit scholarships**. Public and private colleges often award money to outstanding athletes across a variety of sports. Institutions list information on the availability of such scholarships and your student's high school coach as well as the college coach are often excellent resources to speak to when considering playing <u>and</u> paying for a college.

Gift Aid consists of grants or scholarships that do not need to be repaid. **Federal Work-Study (FWS)** is a federally supported program that offers part-time employment for a student and it is based on financial need. **FWS** allows qualified students to work and earn income to pay part of their college expenses. The income is taxable but is not counted by the **FM** or **IM** aid formulas.

Tuition reduction – It is also within the college's realm of decision-making to simply reduce the level of tuition to support a student's ability to afford it. High grade point averages and test scores influence the school's willingness to reduce tuition to entice the student to attend.

7

Education Loans

There are four primary avenues to acquiring financial support in the way of loans to pay for college: **student loans**, **parent loans**, **private loans,** and **alternative loans**. There are advantages and disadvantages to each, so a little explanation is warranted in your education process.

Student loans are taken out by the student rather than the parents, may be subsidized by the state or federal government and are also guaranteed. These loans have interest rates that are usually lower than regular unsecured loans. Repayment is deferred until the student has graduated or left the institution, or becomes less than a half-time student. The student signs a promissory note for these loans that are designed to assist with the **EFC** as well as to help fill the **GAP**.

These loans are one of two types: need-based and non-need based. The need-based **Perkins Loan** program is government money but the school is the lender. This loan is available to undergrads and to graduate students without a parent cosigner. It has an <u>annual</u> undergraduate maximum ($5,500 at 5% rate of interest as of this publication) and repayment begins nine months after graduation. The student has ten years to repay it. The **Perkins Loan** is a very good deal when compared to all other loans we will discuss, but the **Direct Subsidized Stafford Loan** is not far behind in value.

The **Direct Subsidized Stafford Loan** (6.8% with a maximum indebtedness of $23,000 as of this publication) is also based on need. This loan is a good deal because the government pays the interest while the student is in full-time status. Repayment of the loan and interest by the student begins six months after the student either graduates, leaves the institution, or becomes less than a half-time student.

The **Direct Unsubsidized Stafford Loan** (6.8% as of this publication with a $31,000 maximum indebtedness) is not based on need and almost all dependent students who complete the **FAFSA** are eligible to receive one. Interest is charged as soon as the money is disbursed but payments can be made while the student is in school to keep interest from accruing until repayment of principal begins.

A **Stafford Loan** is a part of almost every aid package. Additional **Stafford Loan** money above the limits stated here may be available for dependent students whose parents are unable to qualify for the **Parent Loan for Undergraduate Student (PLUS)** but the extra money provided via **Stafford Loans** must be <u>unsubsidized</u> (total indebtedness not to exceed $57,500).

For more information on current rates and loan limits as well as program changes, see www.studentaid.ed.gov.

College Loans from the institution are sometimes offered as part of the aid package and while some are attractive, others require immediate loan repayments with rates and terms that come close to those of credit card companies. While such a loan may be offered as part of the college aid package, you are not obligated to accept the loan. It is important to review these offers carefully.

Parent Loans are fixed rated loans often referred to as **PLUS (Parent Loan for Undergraduate Student)** (7.9% plus a 4% origination fee as of this publication) which are unsubsidized and based loosely on the parents' financial credit ratings. Interest on these loans begins accruing immediately and unless you seek deferment of those payments through the lender, payments usually start within two months of signing the loan papers.

Note that these **PLUS** loans are designed to help a family pay for its portion of the expenses (**EFC**) as well as the **GAP** (the amount of need not met by the school). The school will often offer a **PLUS** loan in their award letter; however the reality is that there is no free money here, merely a source to get the bills paid. You are still paying it all back with interest.

Private Education Loans are signature student loans that are available from a variety of resources including banks. Some require initial cosigners with rates tied to the prime rate. Annual borrowing limits can be quite high. It is imperative that you read the fine print as it is not uncommon to have the interest rate tied to payment requirements that are often unobtainable. Much like credit card companies, private education loans will often include the right to dramatically increase your interest rate upon a single late payment or other minor infractions of the agreement.

Alternative Loans include home equity lines of credit, traditional mortgage refinancing, mortgage acceleration, loans against life insurance, personal or family loans, margin loans, and even credit card loans.

Home Equity Line of Credit (HELOC) is a type of mortgage, usually in second position behind your first mortgage, structured as a revolving line of credit.

This can be a viable and potentially tax friendly option for families with equity in their homes. If you have good credit the interest rate will likely be competitive with other loan options. The caution on the interest rate is that it is usually variable and can be adjusted monthly, meaning you could see a significant increase in interest rates and consequentially a substantial increase in your payment. The minimum payment on most home equity lines of credit is an interest only payment which may be attractive during the cash flow demanding years of college. Another key in using the equity from your home is to ensure that you have a plan to put the equity back before retirement.

Traditional Mortgage Refinancing may be an attractive alternative source of funds. It involves refinancing your current mortgage, or if your house is paid for, taking out another first mortgage. It may be an option if you have equity in your home, if your current interest rate is higher than current available interest rates, or if you have a current loan that is payable over something less than 30 years. If you have one of these situations, you may find refinancing will either allow you to pull a lump sum of money out or greatly improve cash flow to allow you to pay for some of the college expenses out of pocket. Again, if you entertain the idea of using your home equity you must have a plan to repay prior to retirement.

Mortgage Acceleration Programs (MAP) are not a loan or a source of money to pay for college. Rather, these programs are used to accelerate the repayment of your mortgage in a systematic way. Regardless of whether you are pulling out equity in a lump sum or extending the length of your mortgage to free up monthly cash flow, you must have a plan to replenish that equity prior to your retirement.

By incorporating a **MAP** into your financial plan, you will pay off your mortgage faster, pay less interest over the life of the loan and put yourself in a better position for retirement. There are a few **MAPs** that you may choose from including bi-weekly payments, bi-monthly payments and interest cancellation systems. Debt Planning Relief (www.debtplanningrelief.com) is one of the most cost effective and user friendly mortgage acceleration programs I have found.

Permanent life insurance loans can be a good option. Permanent life insurance provides you the opportunity to use your cash value as collateral to borrow money from the life insurance company at preferred interest rates. This loan does not require good credit or even a job. Another advantage is that you control the payments made as well as the frequency. It is important to read your life insurance policy for details on how loans from your particular policy work.

Family or Personal Loans can be facilitated with family members as well as good personal friends who find themselves in a financial situation to loan money to students they know and trust. Personal loans are often mutually beneficial: the student gets money for school at an attractive interest rate and the lender helps a student and receives a rate of interest greater than a savings account or certificate of deposit might pay. Consult an attorney for guidance in drafting a written agreement.

Margin Loans involve borrowing against your investment account. If you have an investment account with securities that you do not want to sell, either because of the tax consequences or because of the growth potential, you may find it more appealing to borrow against the account. It is important to keep in mind that these securities will be unavailable to you until this loan is paid off. Consult with your investment firm on the amount you may borrow and the interest rate that would be charged.

Loans to Avoid are easily available. While there are other loan possibilities (credit cards, 401k loans, IRA loans, etc.), I generally caution against exercising these options. In most cases you will either pay too high of a price, put your own financial future in jeopardy, or ruin your chance of a comfortable retirement.

One final word on financing college involves a discussion on using military service to help some students reach their goals of an affordable higher education. Not only will military service entitle your teen to education during and after active service, but joining the service after receiving a college degree can result in the government paying some or all of the student loans as a condition of enlistment.

8
Costly Assumptions about Financial Aid

Literally billions of dollars in financial aid are available to those who need help paying for college. Yet, misinformation clouds the facts about what type of aid is available and who is eligible. Here are some costly assumptions about financial aid for college that show why everyone should apply.

College is just too expensive for our family – Cost for college is expensive until you realize that a college graduate earns an average of $1 million more over his/her career than a high-school graduate. There are some expensive schools, but high tuition is not a requirement for a good education. The truth is, not getting a college education can be even more "costly."

There's less aid available than there used to be - The fact is student financial aid has risen to record levels in recent years. Most students receive some form of aid. Less of this money comes in the form of grants and is now usually awarded through low-interest loans. You should consider carefully the financing packages you are offered by each college to determine which makes the most financial sense. Aid is indeed available.

We have too many assets/investments to qualify for aid – Parents who have substantial investments in retirement accounts such as 401(k)s, IRAs, pension programs or the like will often believe that they will not qualify for financial aid. However, under the **Federal Methodology**, retirement accounts do not count against a family.

Our income is too high to qualify for aid - Aid is intended to make a college education available for students of families in many financial situations. College financial aid administrators often take into account not only income, but also other family members in college, home, mortgage costs, and other factors. Aid is awarded to many families with incomes they thought would disqualify them.

We saved for college, so we won't qualify for aid - Saving for college is always a good idea. Since most financial aid comes in the form of loans, the aid you are likely to receive will need to be repaid. Tucking away money could mean you have fewer loans to repay, and it will not necessarily mean you're not eligible for aid if you need it. The key is to identify those types of investment accounts that will not harm your chances of receiving aid and to do so prior to applying for financial aid.

Our debt load situation will help us get financial aid – The fact is that debt is not a factor in determining the amount of aid you receive. They do not care about your house, car and credit card payments, or about any of your other debts. This is why it is imperative to streamline your monthly payments during the "paying for college years" as much as possible.

I'm not a straight "A" student, so I won't receive aid - It's true that many scholarships reward merit, but the vast majority of federal aid is based on financial need and does not even consider grades. Good grades are helpful so it is never too late to raise that GPA, but financial aid is based on need. If you can get into the college of your choice, financial aid may be available to assist.

If I am offered a loan, I have to take it - Families are not obligated to accept any loans awarded to them. Everyone should apply for financial aid via the **FAFSA,** especially since low interest rate loans are available. Compare the rates and repayment plans and take the loan that best meets your needs.

Working will hurt my teen's academic success - Students who attempt to juggle full-time work and full-time studies can struggle. But research shows that students who work a moderate amount often do better academically. Securing an on-campus job related to career goals is a good way for a student to help pay college costs, get experience, and create new ties with the university. Perhaps **Work-Study** or **Co-Op** programs will serve you best.

Private schools are out of financial reach for our family - Finding a college or university program that meets your academic, career, and personal needs is most important. Experts recommend deferring cost considerations until late in the college-selection process. In fact, you might have a better chance of receiving aid from a private school. Private colleges often offer more financial aid to attract students from every income level. Higher college expenses also mean a better chance of demonstrating financial need. A cost comparison may pleasantly surprise you!

Millions of dollars in scholarships go unused every year - Professional scholarship search services often tout this statistic. In fact, most unclaimed money is slated for a few eligible candidates, such as employees of a specific corporation or members of a certain organization. Most financial aid comes from the federal government, though it is also a good idea to research other sources of aid. Make sure you research what is available to you from various resources.

We will have to sell our house to pay for college - Home value is not considered in calculations for federal financial aid. Colleges may take home equity into account when determining how much you are expected to contribute to college costs, but income is a far greater factor in this determination. No college will expect your parents to sell their house to pay for your education. They may turn your room into an exercise room while you are away though!

We can "negotiate" a better deal - Many colleges will be sensitive to a family's specific financial situation, especially if certain nondiscretionary costs, such as unusually high medical bills, job loss or business down-turn, have not typically communicated on the forms submitted. Most colleges adhere to specific financial aid-award guidelines and they will use professional judgment to enhance an award when a need truly exists. They do not view this process however as negotiating.

Financial aid is easy – Applying for financial aid is not difficult, yet most people do not take the time to educate themselves about the process. If you educate yourself and work with experts in the field you will likely be successful.

9

Developing Your Plan:
Basic Beliefs

You have learned a considerable amount about the process of funding a college education. It is time to develop the plan that will allow you to pay for your child's post high school education while maintaining your life style and retirement at the levels you desire. Consider this part of the plan to be like laying out the road map with a solid GPS system so when you want to end up at Disneyland you do not find yourself several hundred miles (dollars) short and in the Mojave Desert!

For now let's assume money is not an issue and make our first question to answer, "What do Mom and

Dad <u>want</u> to pay?" It is quite common for you to not agree at first. I have found about 90% of the adults I work with typically want to follow a path that their parents took with them when it comes to paying for college.

The costs can vary dramatically depending on whether your young adult is staying at home or going away to school, working part-time or not at all. So these are all factors that must be agreed upon to some degree as a plan is first being drafted.

Another factor often overlooked is how <u>much</u> education are you willing to fund? Are you going to help with or pay for the undergraduate degree? For how many years: four, five or longer? It often does take more than four years. Will you pay for any graduate school work? Remember to plan for inflation, as college costs seldom stay the same over four years or more. Consider these components to help you complete the rest of the college funding puzzle.

Some families may end up determining in their plan that they can afford a certain amount of money per year, per child and beyond that their teen(s) will need to assume the cost of college loans they will be obligated to pay back.

Engaging your teen early in this conversation is critical in the planning stages and will reduce stress in the family later. Conversations during the sophomore year in high school or prior are good because college and career choices are usually just being conceptualized for the first time. Once a college is "selected" in a teen's mind it may be tough to make changes and that can reduce the options open to funding college.

So in that perfect world where money is not an issue, you look at distances away from family, cultural and regional similarities or differences with the home town that may ease or stress the transition to a new location, and the size of the college. These points also require some healthy discussions with your young adult whose ideas need to be considered.

Unless money is no obstacle, you must value college as more than a maturational experience. It has become far too expensive to lose sight of the fact that a degree is the end goal of attending college and only in as much as it provides access to a lifetime of opportunity, usually in the form of career choice and greater income.

Once you have some of the basics of the plan determined, it is time to talk facts. Specifically, what can you afford if you are not willing to sacrifice your retirement, and of course that is the premise of this book! If you agree with that, then the rest of this text will continue to make sense to you.

10

Planning – Your Retirement

In order to ensure that your retirement is not put in jeopardy during the "paying for college" years, you must define what you want your retirement to look like and when you want it to happen. Once you have a clear picture of these two key plan components the next important step is to evaluate your financial progress toward meeting those goals.

First, what do you want retirement to look like? As you read this you may already feel that your retirement dream and your retirement reality may not look anything alike. Actually, that is a common sentiment, especially given the recent economic challenges, changes and struggles. However, when examining retirement there are a few pleasant realizations.

Most people desire a retirement lifestyle like what they are currently enjoying, maybe even with another vacation or two added to the annual schedule. People will often jump to the conclusion that they must therefore have an income comparable to what they have now. This is not necessarily the case.

The cost of living does change at retirement for most people. It takes more money to live on prior to retirement than after retirement even to maintain the same standard of living. Certain "costs" disappear at retirement enabling you to live on less.

For example, my wife and I have four children and I see the large percentage of our income that is currently spent on them (private school, clothes, sports, piano lessons, camps, food, saving for college, etc.). Then I note the 15% that we contribute to retirement through a 401(k), permanent life insurance and Roth IRAs. Add in to that the significant portion of our income that goes to pay for our home (which we will have the option to pay off before we retire if we choose). Almost all of those expenses disappear at retirement.

What does that mean? The current percentage of our income spent on our standard of living is only a

Planning - Your Retirement

fraction of our income. In fact, only about 50% of our income goes to maintain <u>our</u> standard of living right now and when those "kid, house and retirement" expenses disappear, we can certainly live on less.

As you define your retirement you need to ask yourself what you want to do: travel, dine out more, or take up golf, tennis or dancing? Whatever this looks like for you, try to assign a cost as if you were doing it today. Then, look at your current budget and remove, like I did above, all of the items that will no longer be expenditures upon retirement. Finally, look at health insurance and prescription costs, for these could add a significant amount to your monthly expenses. Once you have accomplished this, you now should have a fairly accurate picture of what retirement looks like.

For many, once they have estimated their retirement budget and estimated their costs to send their children to school they question the reality of being able to truly do both.

Fewer people are retiring earlier due to the recent economic issues. I personally think this is good. Studies show that a moderate amount of work and stress for people of all ages is good. So I would challenge you to rethink how you define retirement and retirement age.

Perhaps your current job is too taxing, stressful, or physically challenging. Maybe you are just not

~ 61 ~

inspired to do it any longer. Planning your retirement in two stages may be a good solution. The first stage is a point where you have eliminated most or all of your debt. You have saved a sufficient amount however the money still needs time to grow. Consider semi-retirement, working 20 or 30 hours per week at something you enjoy that will pay you enough to cover your bills and maybe provide you with healthcare.

Do not under estimate the value of a part-time job. There are numerous studies that show the importance of both the mental and the physical stimulus that come with working well beyond the normal age of retirement. In fact someone made a statement to me the other day that when you talk with those who are working into their golden years they always appear to be so cheerful. How true!

There is a significant monetary value to part time work. A job of $12.50 per hour for 25 hours would generate $312.50 per week and if you did this 45 weeks per year (allowing for time off for vacation, holidays etc.) it would generate $14,062 per year. This would be the equivalent of an extra $281,250 in an investment account earning 5% income per year for you.

Stage two of retirement may still include working a day or two per week at something you enjoy.

However you are now receiving Social Security and may start taking income from your investments.

Once you have laid out your plan it is time to use one or more of the excellent retirement projection tools available. Just like any software program, the value of a retirement projection is only going to be as good as the data put in to it. So it is best to start with good, accurate data. The key inputs are going to include: current investments for retirement, retirement age, inflation rate, income needed at retirement, sources of income (i.e. Social Security and pension) and rate of return on investments prior to and during retirement.

I would like to comment on a few of these as their accuracy is important to the outcome. Inflation has been relatively low for the last couple of decades but it still cannot be overlooked. For example at only three percent inflation, a $65,000 per year standard of living today will require just over $118,000 per year in 20 years. Over the last 30 years the average rate of inflation has been just over four percent.

Many mistakes are made by individuals when they calculate the rate of return on their investments prior to retirement. This happens because the majority of the software programs ask for "average rate of return" to calculate the future retirement balances. "Average" can be a serious misleading calculation as you will see with this short quiz.

Quiz: A two-year "average" return of 10% on $100,000 would result in which balance at the end of two years?

(a) $121,000   (b) $112,000   (c) $105,000

The answer is that they are **all** correct. In (a) it was a flat 10% return per year. In (b) the investment lost 20% in year one and gained 40% in year two for an average of 10% gain overall and in (c) the investment lost 30% in year one and gained 50% in year two.

Year 1 Rate of Return	End of Year 1 Balance	Year 2 Rate of Return	End of Year 2 Balance	**Average Return for 2 Years**
10%	$ 110,000	10%	$ 121,000	**10%**
(20%)	$ 80,000	40%	$ 112,000	**10%**
(30%)	$ 70,000	50%	$ 105,000	**10%**

The lesson here should be clear: you must be very careful when using "average" rates of return. It is probably wise to input a more conservative number in your planning.

Another cautionary point with the calculation inputs is the rate of taxation that you will be paying at retirement. A dangerous assumption is often made that you will automatically be in a lower tax bracket at retirement. One reason this is often inaccurate is that many times people are living on less income at retirement but they have lost many of their deductions and exemptions (i.e. the children and the home mortgage) so these two will cancel each other out leaving them with the same amount of taxable income.

Another reason to be cautious and conservative with inputting numbers into the calculations is the current amount of government spending taking place in this country today. Regardless of your political perspective on the effectiveness of the money that the government has spent in order to stabilize the economy in the United States, there is without question an almost larger than comprehendible debt that must be paid in the future. I, along with many others, believe that this may come in the form of much higher personal income tax rates. This would have a significant impact on retirement incomes.

Once you have entered all of your figures you will want to be able to adjust the various inputs to see how each will impact your retirement picture. For example, adjusting the rate of return by one or two percentage points or delaying retirement by a year or two can both have substantial changes on how long your money will last.

Regardless of what tool you use, the key is to be able to extract from the data how much of your income you will need to contribute to retirement and what amount of your investments you can afford to use to pay for college. Being prepared with this information will greatly increase the likelihood of not putting retirement at risk as you plan and pay for the college years.

11

Planning for the Cost

According to the **National Center for Education Statistics** for the 2010/11 school year, the annual cost of attendance **(COA)** of a private school was just over $39,518 and for a public college it was just about $17,860.* Those costs have increased between one and two times the rate of inflation and continue to rise at the rate of four to six percent each year. The following chart shows how an increase of five percent impacts cost for one child over five years.

Public school costs vary greatly from state to state and could be considerably higher or lower than the national average stated here.

Year in School	COA with 5% Increase Per Year	Aggregate Cost
2013-2014	30,000	30,000
2014-2015	31,500	61,500
2015-2016	33,075	94,575
2016-2017	34,729	129,304
2017-2018	36,465	165,769

Families with multiple children will need to include all of them in their projection in order to get a complete picture of what their total outlay is likely to be. Here is an example using my family. Let's assume two of my four children will go to private universities graduating in 4 years and two will go to public universities graduating in 5 years, beginning in 2013.

Four Moffitt Children in College from 2014 to 2025				
Child College Years	Annual Cost (Inflation Adjusted to Year Starting College)	Cost Each Year	Total Cost for Degree	Estimated Cost Per Year for Moffitt College (# in college)
Mary Public 5 Years	$18,406	**14** $18,406 **15** $19,326 **16** $20,292 **17** $21,307 **18** $22,372	$107,703	**2014** $18,406 **2015** $19,326 **2016** $40,584 (2) **2017** $42,614 (2) **2018** $44,744 (2)
Alex Public 5 Years	$20,292	**16** $20,292 **17** $21,307 **18** $22,372 **19** $23,491 **20** 24,666	$112,128	**2019** $70,769 (2) **2020** $74,307 (2) **2021** $104,246(2) **2022** $109,460(2) **2023** $57,466 (1) **2024** $60,340 (1)

Child College Year	Annual Cost (Inflation Adjusted to Year Starting College)	Cost Each Year	Total Cost for Degree	
Andrew Private 4 Years	$50,567	**19** $47,278 **20** $49,641 **21** $52,123 **22** $54,730	$203,772	
Anna Private 4 Years	$52,123	**21** $52,123 **22** $54,730 **23** $57,466 **24** $60,340	$224,659	**Grand Total** 642,262

So school shopping, based on a variety of factors you have identified as important, is an excellent idea. Twenty colleges that can deliver what you are seeking allow you to focus on those and begin your in-depth investigation and then the application process to increase the likelihood that one or more will provide you with the good financial package you desire.

Obviously the cost will be impacted tremendously by the college and career chosen so I must provide you with some tough love information before I proceed any further. I will give you a couple of examples to illustrate some essential points about the pre-selection process.

A friend of mine told me it would have been worth the $12,000 a year more to send his daughter to a private school for a degree in occupational therapy than the state school where his wife insisted their daughter attend. His reasoning was based on the "name recognition" of the school.

I pointed out to him that the job market for occupational therapists has been at an all time high with many receiving sign-on bonuses to take jobs. Her quality education at the state school walked her into a job even before graduation so that extra $48,000 dad was willing to finance would have been wasted money.

However, there are cases where the reputation of a college is very important and should be a vital factor in the selection process. This applies to the student who is planning to go to medical school, the student who achieves at very elite academic levels and plans to go to graduate school, or the student with a major in studies that will lead to a very unique or specialized profession. So, in some situations, college "name" does make a difference.

Criminology is currently one of the fields of study in high demand. It is widely believed that this is due to the CSI (Criminal Scene Investigation) series of television shows. The "Hollywood" or "big screen" versions of many careers fail to truly depict the life of a person with the real world job. The truth is that while those careers are very important to our society the vast majority of them lack the glitz and glitter portrayed on television. Once that is realized it usually means a change in degree major which certainly leads to additional time in college and an increase in costs.

That is why I strongly encourage students in their last three years of high school to do career interviews, job shadowing, as well as serious research into what careers may interest them. Spend a day in the career and make sure the positive and the negative aspects of the work are discussed. Job elimination is just as important as job selection!

They should talk to friends, neighbors, as well as church and family members in different careers, and spend some time with the high school counselor who can help to suggest career paths based on the interest and skills of the teen. Even if a career has been "chosen" encourage constant exploration before registering for college. Changing careers and degree majors are usually the number one causes of extending the number of years in college and that means increasing the costs.

Leaving the choice of a college major and subsequently a career selection up to chance is simply a luxury most families cannot afford. Career interviews and job shadowing will certainly increase the likelihood of making proper choices. However, adding an even more scientific approach called personality profiling to this process can significantly increase the odds of selecting a proper major as well as a career in which an individual will thrive.

There are many choices in personality profiling tests yet for the past 50 years the *Birkman Method*© has been an industry leader and my personal preference. This tool measures usual behaviors, underlying needs, stress behaviors and multiple hard wired personality traits. The personality results, when coupled with a student's academic profile, will allow for a laser-like focus on career and major choices that really make sense. For more information on the *Birkman Method*© go to www.collegeplanningrelief.com.

In the process of selecting an appropriate major and career it is important to have the "money talk." Most students have limited information on how much a job or career pays, and perhaps more importantly, they have little idea what standard of living that the career might afford them.

Many of you will recall the Cosby Show from the late 1980's: a sitcom about the "Huxtable family" with mom an attorney and dad a physician rearing five school age children. There is a particular episode with the dad, Bill Cosby, and the high school son Theo that every parent should watch.

Dr. Huxtable is sitting on his son's bed discussing the importance of a good college education. Theo tells his Dad, "I don't want to be like you and Mom. I just want to be regular people." Dad, looks at him, goes to the Monopoly game sitting on a shelf and asks Theo, "How much do you suppose regular folk will make per week?" Theo says, "How about $250?" Dad grins and says, "Here is $300." Theo smiles saying, "$1,200 per month is great!" Dad immediately takes back $350 for taxes, $200 for transportation, $300 for rent, 100 for clothes. Theo says, "Take $200, I want to look good!" Theo smiles at his father, thinking he has proven his point. Holding up the remaining money, he says, "See Dad, no problem! " Dr. Huxtable immediately takes half of the last small amount of cash and says, "You haven't eaten yet! Still smiling Dr. H asks one final question, "Are you going to have a girl friend?" Theo smiles, sits back and says, "Of course!" Dad takes the rest of the money!

Many of our children have been blessed to grow up with privileges such as large houses, nice cars and fabulous vacations, but their chosen career path may not bring to them those same niceties. We want our children to follow their dreams and we know that money is not everything but we certainly want our children to know the financial realities.

12

Navigating College Costs

Comparing college to college has become much easier thanks to the Internet and software programs. One excellent resource tool available to families is *College Cost Navigator* (*CCN*) that not only provides you with detailed financial comparison reports but also succinctly lays out specific data regarding each school.

What is so useful about the *CCN* is that it goes well beyond the financial comparisons and provides you with information on each college's enrollment numbers, admission requirements, basis for candidate selection, admission procedures, a freshman class profile (the range of ACT/SAT scores of admitted students), student body characteristics (in vs. out of state, race, average age of full-time undergraduates, percent seeking degrees, etc.), financial aid as well as scholarships and grants. Critical telephone contact numbers are also included.

Available comparison information on each school also includes data on loans available, student employment, academic accreditation, degree offerings, majors leading to a bachelor's degree, academic requirements and programs, facilities, percentage of returning students, guidance and student services.

Many students are interested in knowing about the intercollegiate sports as well as the intramural and recreational athletic programs. *CCN* includes all of that in the college profiles. For students who want to get involved in student activities and organizations from the school newspaper to the honor societies, the *CCN* includes those as well.

Other comparison information includes housing requirements, general regulations, transportation availability, the school calendars and orientation information for freshmen.

The *College Cost Navigator* can be "test driven" by going to www.collegecostnavigator.com and downloading the trial sample.

13

Costs in College Selection

Changing colleges can lead to significant cost increases, so the college selection process should be approached in a systematic way. Students switch schools more often due to factors <u>other than </u>course work for a career or degree change. Geographic proximity and what that means in terms of time and travel between school and home, especially with many colleges closing their dorms over breaks, has caused many young adults to change schools so home/school travel is not a burden in time and/or money.

Likewise, factors including socialization, difficulty of the class work, student/faculty ratios, etc. may cause a first or second year "re-evaluation" that results in a school change/transfer. Transfers are seldom efficient since not all completed coursework may transfer, especially if switching when semester/quarter programs are involved. Also, classes that were paid for and successfully completed may have no value to the new institution.

There is a psychological theory called primacy-recency that must be addressed in order to ensure a quality and successful school selection experience. With respect to college visits, primacy-recency suggests that a student will have the sharpest memories of his/her first college visit and the most recent college visit with all other visits ending up in a melded blur.

To overcome that effect, I believe it is critical to use the same score sheet for every school visit so the attributes of each college can be rated, and in the end, the colleges can be ranked based on the weighted criteria you have established.

I have identified over two dozen criteria that help in the selection of a college and increase the likelihood that a student will stay there for his/her college years. The higher the score the greater the compatibility there will be between the student and college. The evaluation charts used during college visits allow the student to rank and then rate criteria so there can be scores to compare schools when all the investigations have been concluded. You can create your own chart for your family.

There is considerable data available on colleges including the historical rate of inflation for their tuition and room and board, as well as how many years it typically takes for a student in a particular program to earn the degree. That information is helpful as you plan what the true cost of attendance is for a particular school and degree program.

If the college selection process is done carefully with website investigation, on-site visits while classes are in session, visiting dorms and speaking with current students, asking the right questions, observing activities, and many other factors, you will be able to rate each college's overall performance based on your personalized scoring.

When you systematically review the colleges by comparing all of the important criteria prior to submitting the applications you will be able to ascertain the true **Cost of Attendance** of each school.

14

Expected Family Contribution - Strategies to Reduce

Your expected family contribution (**EFC**) will initially be determined by the "base year" information you provide on the **FAFSA** form or **CSS Profile Form**. That base year is the last complete calendar year prior to the first year of college which means it includes the last half of the junior year in high school and the first half of the senior year.

The base year not only establishes your family's financial aid package for the freshman year in college but it also sets the precedent for your family's package thereafter. Radical changes in your financial picture would more than likely be needed in order to substantially change that financial aid structure.

If you are going to take any actions to lower your **EFC** then your opportunity is prior to December 31 of your teen's junior year in high school. Prior to that deadline you will need to estimate your **EFC** and identify potential colleges your student is interested in attending. That information will then give you an idea if financial aid might be available to you.

If you have determined that aid may be a possibility, then maximizing aid opportunities in that base year is your next step. This includes tax planning as an important part of this process. However this is not your ordinary tax planning. In fact you will try to reduce both your income and your itemized deductions because the goal is to *minimize* base year income, but then *maximize* the tax paid. I am not suggesting that I want you to pay more in taxes however I am suggesting that your tax savings be deferred to the following year.

If your job provides you a year-end bonus, you may ask your employer to defer this income out of the base year and into the new, non-base year. While you will likely only delay your income for a matter of weeks you may avoid that income being counted as a part of your expected family contribution.

Similarly, if you make only eleven mortgage payments in the base year it will increase your taxes by reducing your interest expense deduction therefore causing your **EFC** to decrease. You do that by making the January payment in that base year back in December and by not taking your January payment for the next year in December of your base year.

In a similar manner if you consolidate charitable contributions into the years before and after the base year it will be to your advantage. A charitable contribution lowers tax liability and increases your net income in the calculations. That has a negative impact on your **EFC**. Move such contributions out of the base year and they have a positive influence on your **EFC**.

It is best not to sell securities during the base year. Any capital gains earned from a sale will increase your income and will cause a corresponding rise in your **EFC**. If you must sell an investment, it is wise to offset the capital gain with a loss from another investment. You may also be able to avoid the gain if you borrow against the investment until after the base year. If you sell investments with capital or short-term losses it will reduce that base year income. Losses can be used to offset an equal amount of long-term capital gains or up to $3,000 of ordinary income.

Not all investment accounts are treated the same in the calculations so it is important to review each carefully. All retirement accounts (401k, IRA, 403b, SIMPLE plans and annuities) are protected and not factored in to either the **Federal** or **Institutional Methodologies**. (The federal methodology also allows for an asset protection on included investments.

In all of these cases, any contributions you make to those retirement accounts in that base year are added back to your income for the **EFC** calculations. This asset protection allowance in a two parent household is the approximate age of the oldest parent less 10 in thousands of dollars. If Dad at 45 is the older parent then the family would have approximately $35,000 of assets other than retirement that would not count in the calculation. In a single parent household the asset protection allowance is less than half of that of the two-parent family. If the single parent is 45, the allowance is $14,900.

Assets like mutual funds, stocks, and certificates of deposit that are earmarked for retirement may serve you better if they are moved to investment accounts like the ones mentioned previously that do not count against you. Always consider the costs, taxes and penalties you may incur if you make such a move, as well as the IRS limitations placed on the availability of those funds until age 59½. Check your particular plan before making a withdrawal.

Permanent life insurance (PLI) is an option that offers some greater opportunities because it can provide you with access to and control of your money while potentially avoiding unnecessary taxation and visibility on the financial aid forms. **PLI** is not typically known for its investment characteristics or rates of return but when designed properly the return will be better than a savings account, is guaranteed, and does not count in many of the financial calculations for determining aid. Always work with an insurance company with high ratings and insurance plans designed for such a purpose.

It is possible to have a zero **EFC** if your household income is below $24,000 if you qualify to file the 1040EZ or 1040A. In those cases you automatically receive a zero **EFC** regardless of assets that you may own. If you are permitted, it may be advantageous to file such tax forms, even if you have to forego some tax opportunities. Again, it will be necessary to weigh those potential tax losses against what you will receive in financial aid.

15

Maximizing Aid Opportunities

As you begin the process of identifying the schools to apply to, it is important to bring into the financial equation the aid packages that will be offered. By this point you and your teen should have the profiles of the types of schools that are in consideration. Now you review the various financial components of each college to see how they will impact your family's share of the cost of attendance.

Start with the **Cost of Attendance (COA)** to determine whether or not aid is an option for you at this school. **Need** is equal to **COA** minus **EFC.** If you have a **NEED** at a particular institution you will want to next review their percentage of need met. Just because you have a need does not mean that the school will meet that need for you. For example, with a college **COA** of $30,000 per year and your **EFC** of $12,000, your need is $18,000. If the school only meets 60% of that need then it will provide you with aid of $10,800 thus leaving you an **unmet need** or **gap** of $8,200. This is <u>added</u> to your **EFC** ($12,000) for a total first year out of pocket of $20,200, which is much more than your **EFC**.

Conversely, a school that meets 90% of need in the same situation as above will provide your family aid of $16,200 only adding $1,800 to your **EFC** of $12,000 for a total out of pocket of $13,800. This is quite a difference between two schools with the same **COA**.

The difference in the need met between those two schools with the same **COA** is $5,400 <u>per year</u>. Over five years that is a total of $27,000 in more aid from the school that meets the higher need. Even if 50% of that came in the form of gift money (money that did not require repayment) you would be saving over $13,500.

Next, consider the makeup of the **financial aid award**. Not all financial aid is created equally. Some schools will meet the **NEED** in the form of loans while others will do so in the form of grants and scholarships. Obviously you are looking for schools that will provide a higher percentage of aid in the form of grant money as opposed to loans or work study.

Private institutions tend to have more money available than public colleges to provide for financial need. This money comes largely from their endowment funds. This key difference between public and private schools will often narrow the gap between an "expensive" private school and a "cheap" public school.

This is also the time to review the average length of time to obtain a four year degree at the colleges on your list. If the average length of time is closer to six years then you very well may be increasing your costs by 50% (six years instead of four). Schools with an average closer to four years to graduate with a strong financial aid package that meets most of your need and does so in the form of free money may be your best financial option even if its sticker price is considerably higher than other schools with greater financial aid but with longer graduation times.

Let's look at an example of two schools: an expensive school and a cheaper school. The family that we will use in this comparison has an **EFC** of $12,000. Remember, your family's <u>situation</u> plays a role in which school may have the right financial aid package for you.

School A (the expensive school) has a **COA** of $35,000 per year. School B (the cheaper school) has a **COA** of $18,000 or 51% of the more expensive college. Given the large difference in cost between the two, many people might believe that a comparison is not even worth the time. How could it make a difference?

School A meets 100% of the need and does so with 90% in gift aid and only 10% in loans. At a cost of $35,000 and an **EFC** of $12,000, it leaves us with a need of $23,000. Of that amount only $2,300 is in student loans. Add that to our **EFC** and we arrive at a total out of pocket of $14,300.

School B meets 60% of a family's need and 50% of that is in the form of gift aid. With a **COA** of $18,000 and the **EFC** of $12,000 we arrive at a need of $6,000 with $3,600 of that being met and 50% of that being a loan ($1,800). If we add up our out of pocket we have: $12,000 **EFC** + $2,400 of unmet need + $1,800 in loans for a total of $16,200. This is $1,900 **MORE** at the cheaper school than at School A, the more expensive school which had a cost that was almost double to start!

School A ("Expensive")		School B ("Cheap")	
	COA $35,000		COA $18,000
-	EFC 12,000	-	EFC 12,000
=	Need $23,000	=	Need $ 6,000

School A	School B
100% Need Met	**60% Need Met**
90% Gift 20,700	50% Gift 1,800
10% Loan 2,300	50% Loan 1,800
$ 23,000	$ 3,600

	School A		School B
	Need $23,000		Need $ 6,000
-	Need Met 23,000	-	Need Met 3,600
=	Unmet Need $0	=	Unmet Need $2,400

EFC	$ 12,000	**EFC**	$ 12,000
+ Loans	2,300	+ Loans	1,800
Unmet Need	0	Unmet Need	2,400
Out of Pocket	$14,300	**Out of Pocket**	$16,200

Over four years that additional yearly expense
($1,900) of the "cheaper" school would have cost
your family $7,600. It could have been even a larger
difference if we assume that school B, the cheaper
school, averages five years for a four-year degree
while school A only takes four years. Now we have to
add the cost of a fifth year at school B. Without taking
any inflation into account that would be an additional
$16,200. Add that to the $7,600 for the greater

expense in the first four years and now we are at an increased expense of $23,800. This definitely does not look like School B is less costly than School A!

Your investigation and analysis of the schools on your list is critical to determine which college will be the most cost effective for your family. This is not to suggest that your entire decision should be based exclusively on cost, however the reality is that the research you do will often allow more schools to be considered that otherwise may have been prematurely excluded due to their original sticker price.

16

Your "Paying for College" Team

As I have discussed on numerous occasions throughout this book, the need for a plan to successfully navigate through the college years without jeopardizing retirement is critical. The development of that plan requires multiple team members and experts.

Students – Input, participation and direction from the pre-college teen is essential. After all, the college part of this plan is all about him or her. It is critical to engage the student in all aspects of the process and to do so early. This includes discussions of the financial aspects of the plan and a working understanding of financial aid.

The student should know if Mom and Dad will qualify for assistance, what colleges will maximize the aid and how the balance of the money, that is acquired through loans, will be paid back. If it has not been done previously, this is a great time to begin real world lessons on finances.

Your teen should also be made aware of the financial impact of his/her GPA and test scores. If scholarships are an option it should be his/her responsibility to actively pursue those opportunities. Personally contacting the colleges of interest is also a student responsibility. I have spoken to numerous admission officers and all have the same desire to hear from the students and not their parents. If you are a "helicopter parent," hovering over every move your teen makes, limit your direct involvement with the schools for it will not help the process.

Parents – Mom and Dad need to have a working understanding of the processes involved so that you can explain to your teen the guidelines and timeframes that need to be met. Also, it is your responsibility to keep your college bound youngster on task! Now is not the time to allow a teenager to miss a deadline that may cost the family thousands of dollars.

You will also need to clearly communicate with your student what your financial commitment will be, what his/her financial commitment will be, as well as your expectations for grade production in order for your financial support to continue. Families that reward bad behavior and poor grades rarely find that it ends well financially. This is a heavy investment in your teen's future so if "readiness" for college responsibilities is in question, maybe your financial contributions should come a year or so later when studying may be taken more seriously.

Financial Advisor- If you have an existing relationship with a financial advisor, you need to have a candid conversation with him/her about the training and experience he/she has received in short-term college planning. While this is becoming a much more recognized need in the financial planning community, only a fraction of advisors have any formal education, professional training and actual experience in this area. If yours does not have that background, you may want to search for an individual who can help you with the college process as well as with your finances because much of what you are doing during the paying for college years is counter intuitive to traditional long-term planning. A financial advisor without the background and training in short-term college planning may question the strategies required to maximize aid for college.

Guidance Counselors- Far too often these professionals are expected to do too much and be experts in too many areas. It is not uncommon for a

GC to have a ratio of 1 to 300 students or more. College planning is but one of many areas for which GCs are responsible. They are also class schedulers, career consultants, problem solvers and much more. Find out what your student's school offers in the way of college planning. Recognize that your GC will help your teen find information on various schools, notify them of SAT and ACT test dates and possibly arrange for school visits.

Financial Aid Officers (FAOs) - These are the individuals who you will be communicating with at the college's financial aid offices. They are an important member of your team in this process if financial aid is going to be a part of paying for college. It is important to understand how they will be helpful. They will be able to provide you all of the details about the forms that need to be turned in and when. They are also able to inform you about the composition of the aid package that you are likely to receive. Please remember however that they are employed by the college. Therefore they are not likely to share with you that another school, a competing school, might be able to provide you a better offer. Probably the single greatest benefit that they offer is the ability to listen to your family's story which may include any extenuating circumstances you have. They can use that information and their professional judgment to enhance your financial aid package. I believe it is important enough to mention again that these communications need to come from the applying student, not the parents.

Admissions Officers (AO) - These are the people at the institutions your teen is making application to and who have the ultimate "yes" or "no" say on entrance to the college. The student needs to develop a dialog and relationship with the **AO** even though there may not be a lot of communications coming from those gatekeepers. In most cases, the **AO** is looking at many more applications than openings available. The student must find ways to demonstrate his/her desire to attend that institution and why the **AO** should select him/her.

ACT /SAT Preparation Companies- The difference of a few points on either test can have a definite impact on acceptance or denial to an institution of choice. Also, the same holds true with regard to merit based aid. A slight increase in test scores may increase the amount of aid by thousands of dollars. There are many companies and classes offered to prepare a student to take these tests and to perform at his/her highest levels. The key to being successful here is to establish a baseline score. In other words, the tests are taken the first time without the class or training. This will establish the baseline as well as help identify where the time and specific attention need to be placed.

There are national companies as well as local ones that specialize in preparing students to take the tests. Items to consider include: price, size of classes, and the time when the class is offered relative to the time of the test. Also, you will want to find out if your student can audit the prep class if desired for a third pass at the exam. Finally I believe you should talk with the company about what realistic expectations exist for increasing your child's test scores.

Tutor- This may sound like a strange person to have on your paying for college team however if your student is doing well with the exception of one or two academic areas you may want to consider getting some specialized attention to boost that lagging area. Again this can make a difference between getting in and getting free money. Start with the guidance counselor to see what is available at the school. Check with the ACT/SAT companies who generally offer tutoring as well.

High School Coach- If your child has a desire to play a sport at the collegiate level which may afford him/her some additional aid and/or scholarships you will want to get some help from the high school or club coach. Those individuals can provide excellent help in terms of focusing on the appropriate level of play, for not every high school athlete is ready for prime time. There are however, plenty of schools that he/she will enjoy playing for who may offer some financial rewards to athletes.

Do not waste time focusing on schools that show little interest in your teen. Also, ask the high school coach if he/she will contact the colleges for your athlete and send game video and letters on your teen's behalf. Most high school coaches are part-time coaches with full-time jobs so they will likely have limited time to assist, but you do want to know how they can and will help.

College Athletic Advisor- In the last ten years it has become more popular to hire your own coach to "market" your teen's athletic skills to an array of colleges than to rely on the high school coach to do so for you. This specialist helps you to communicate with the schools, creates videos for you to send, evaluates offers you receive and guides you with his/her knowledge of the college athletic programs. A couple national companies offer this service and have local representatives. Fees range from a few hundred to thousands of dollars. The high school coach and parents of other teens who have used the services can provide you with background on what you will receive for your fees.

FAFSA Prep- There are companies that offer to prepare and submit your **FAFSA** and **CSS Profile** forms for you. Fees range from $75 to $200 per year depending on what they need to submit. As a general rule these are forms that you are able to complete yourself. However, many families would rather pay a fee to have an expert submit these documents to reduce the likelihood of errors and omissions.

Certified Public Accountant (CPA) - Certain tax opportunities may exist for you with a child going off to college. A **CPA** can tell you if these options are available to you. Many people also rely on their **CPA** to help them strategize for that important base year planning. Like financial advisors, there are only a fraction of **CPAs** who have this specialized training. Make sure your **CPA** has knowledge in this area. He or she may need to work with your **Financial Advisor**.

It is certainly possible to accomplish this successfully on your own. However I believe your chances of success increase exponentially with the addition of each quality team member. It has been my experience in life that no matter what I might be doing I am at my best when I have surrounded myself with high quality, knowledgeable professionals.

I grew up watching in amazement and awe as Michael "Air" Jordan (your kids will know him as the guy from *Space Jam*) defied gravity and opponents for years: arguably the best basketball player to play the game. It was so natural and it came so easily to him.

However throughout his career he had three coaches: a shooting coach, a strength coach and his team coach. If Air Jordan can benefit from coaching maybe your family can as well.

17

SAGE Scholars Tuition Rewards

In 1997 SAGE (Savings and Growth for Education) was formed by visionary leaders with higher education experience to help make the cost of college more affordable. It brings together families, colleges and universities, and investment companies to create college funding solutions. SAGE is a college savings plan like no other in the country and is well worth my time and yours to tell you about it.

Families and students earn tuition points for saving for and learning about college. Those tuition discount points accumulate over time and when a student enters college each point is worth one dollar towards the tuition at private colleges and universities across the USA.   Those points can add up to a full year of tuition for each child in a family. SAGE Tuition Reward Points must be spread equally over all four college years.

Tuition Reward Points accrue like frequent flyer miles and are earned by saving with SAGE financial partners who have 529 plans, CDs, mutual funds, annuities, life insurance and even brokerage accounts. These rewards even grow annually at a rate of 5% on eligible assets.

The program is actually quite simple. It starts with 500 points for meeting with a SAGE financial partner to learn about the program. Then, for every $10,000 invested, with no minimum limit, another 500 tuition reward points are awarded. Invest $20,000 and earn 1,000 Tuition Reward Points. The reward points accrue at 5% annually.

Obviously the earlier a family starts the more opportunity it has to earn higher discounts for college. A student must be registered in SAGE by the end of the junior year to receive any benefits. Tuition reward points can only be used at private colleges that accept them. (go to www.tuitionrewards.com) for a list of participating schools.

Let's take a brief look at how a family with one child accumulated $32,174 SAGE points by starting in the program with their sixth grader. The family started with $50,000 in an account and added $10,000 to it each year for the next six years. As a senior, the student has $137,786 with 32,174 SAGE Tuition Reward Points!

Grade Level in School	Deposits	Deposits Plus %5 Growth	SAGE Points
6th	50,000	50,000	
7th	10,000	62,500	2,500
8th	10,000	76,125	3,725
9th	10,000	90,431	3,806
10th	10,000	105,452	4,521
11th	10,000	121,225	5,872
12th	10,000	137,736	6,061
TOTALS	110,000	137,736	32,174

So, in addition to their own "savings" this family has 32,174 SAGE Tuition Reward Points that can be used to reduce the student's annual tuition at a participating SAGE college or university by $8,043 a year! Make sure you ask your financial planner about SAGE Tuition Scholars.

18

Alternative College and Career Solutions

Paying for an undergraduate degree was a large undertaking even before the recent economic woes. Uncertainties in the financial atmosphere have brought about a profound change in how we look at paying for college. It is an unfortunate reality for some families that college is no longer an option due to money concerns. Others find paying for college now requires a major recalibration of their financial plan to keep post high school education a possibility.

Regardless of how this economy has impacted you and your family, there are reasons why you might consider an alternative route to transitioning your teen from a high school student to a contributing adult member of society. This is where there needs to be even more discussion among the parents, the student(s), and other members of your "paying for college" team.

It might be because he/she is not ready in the maturation process for college. He may not be ready to move away from home or she may have no idea what she wants to do. It might also be that there are better job opportunities that do not involve a college education. Below are some alternatives that very well may save the family thousands of dollars as well as put your teen on a successful career path.

The United States military is an option that is worth considering if your son/daughter has expressed some interest in the armed forces. The GI bill grants $47,566 dollars worth of college education benefits in exchange for a 3 year military commitment and a $100 per month reduction in pay. This is considered a veteran's benefit and is actually available when the tour of duty has ended. In addition, while in the service, soldiers are provided 100% tuition assistance. Given the current job market, this does provide a young adult with immediate income while learning a skill or trade that very well may assist him/her in finding employment after military service, especially if college is not an immediate interest.

There is demand today for technical, civil service, trade, medical and health care assistants. These jobs often do not require a four-year college degree. Some examples include: veterinary technicians, medical and dental assistants, physical therapy assistants, environmental engineering technicians, firefighters, police, cosmetologists, as well as many others. Each typically requires a license, technical training or certification but generally speaking the training/education takes less than a couple of years and comes at a fraction of the cost of a traditional four-year college education. There are many rewarding professions like these that will lead to successful careers, especially if your teen shows a strong passion for or interest in them. Additional education and training can always come later using this base career/education as a stepping stone.

Accelerating course work by taking college classes during the summer is another way to reduce the overall expense of a higher education. Summer courses can be taken either at the university where the young adult is enrolled or at a community college that has reciprocity with the targeted four-year institution. Taking summer classes allows a student to finish a degree earlier which eliminates some college expenses and allows entrance into the job market earlier.

Commuting to school may be an option for some students. While there is still a cost to Mom and Dad of that child staying at home, it costs much less than paying for room and board at the school. By doing this for even a year or maybe two, it is possible to reduce expenses by tens of thousands of dollars. Your child could then move onto campus after year one or two and still have plenty of time to experience the college life.

If full-time attendance is out of financial reach, going to school part-time while working may be another viable option that many families might consider. Numerous people have stated how much more they appreciated their education and degree earned after working their way through school. There is something to be said for a strong work ethic developed on the job while attending college.

Community colleges no longer have the stigma they once had of being the schools that offered lesser quality education for lower quality students. Today these beautiful campuses are conveniently located and offer high quality instruction and flexible schedules to meet the needs of young adults on the go. Most community colleges offer more than the basic education requirements and have agreements with universities so that credits and two-year degrees transfer easily to four-year institutions.

The best part of community college is that the education is obtained at a fraction of the price it would have cost at a four-year institution. Once your child has two years of community school education he/she can transfer to a selected university with 50% of the class load completed and a fraction of the money spent. Upon graduation from the four-year institution, there is no asterisk on the degree that says "this student only attended our school for two years." You have spent considerably less for that quality education. The discount with this approach can be as great as 70% compared to an equivalent curriculum at a four-year institution!

Other alternatives are available while your student is in high school. Some states allow high school students to take college classes for free while still in high school. Many students have their high school schedules adjusted to allow them to take basic college courses and then upon high school graduation, already have some required courses completed.

Advanced Placement (AP) classes have several significant benefits for a high school student who is ready to take on the challenges. They are considered "weighted" which means that they are worth more than a typical class on a 4.0 scale which can aid in the college acceptance process. Additionally **AP** classes are comparable to college classes. They require more work and greater attention therefore helping to prepare the future college student for the more rigorous requirements of a college level class.

Another significant benefit of an AP class is financial. The **College Board** offers **AP** exams in a variety of subjects that allow the student who has taken these high school classes the opportunity to "test out" of college classes. Taking and passing these exams allows the student to receive credit for college courses. It is possible for a student to get credit for the entire freshman year of college through this process.

A word of caution is necessary: **AP** classes are very demanding and a student may easily become overloaded with too much work based on the course load and extra-curricular activities. Talk with the school guidance counselor about the appropriate amount, if any, of **AP** classes to take.

College Level Examination Program (CLEP) is the most widely recognized program in the United States for allowing high school students to test out of college classes and receive credit for doing so. Unlike the **AP** process, anyone can participate in the **CLEP** program and can take exams in a variety of subjects. It would be possible for a student to test out of his/her first two years of college.

The **CLEP** process is also administered by **The College Board**. There are registration and testing fees for each exam however the cost is less than $75 per subject, far less than the cost of a college course. For more information, go to www.collegeboard.org.

You may want to also consider working with a local tutor or testing company to have your teen prepare for these exams. Money spent on a tutor and testing fees will still be a fraction of the cost compared to the actual expense of the college courses.

The time value of money also needs to be considered with the **AP** exams and **CLEP** tests. A student who finishes college a year or two early is afforded an opportunity to enter the work force and earn money sooner. It also avoids the last year or two of college which are the most expensive due to inflation.

Another option that is becoming even more popular is on-line education, often referred to as distance learning. In this process, classes are taken on-line with assignments, class "discussions," and "lectures" all done through the internet. Many schools are now offering this option in a variety of areas and levels of education. For the student not interested in attending the traditional school and who is disciplined enough to work in a less supervised environment, the on-line process may be attractive.

It is tempting to believe that everyone must immediately begin at a four-year college and start a degree program right after high school in order to acquire some level of professional success. Families should not feel pressured to follow that traditional route if it just is not right at that time for their student.

College is a great path for many students after high school, but there are many other alternatives. Each student should have a post high school plan that is designed specifically for him or her. To some, that may mean delaying college for a year or two and working, while for others it may mean defending our country in the military and delaying further education. For others, it may mean working part-time and taking classes at a local community college or becoming a skilled member of the work force with training as a firefighter or a nurse assistant. It is "having a plan" that is important.

19

Merit Based Awards

Students with good academic track records have multiple opportunities to be rewarded for their successes. Yes, <u>good</u> academic history is often all that is needed: not great grades and test scores. Families of students with GPAs of 3.0 or greater and an outstanding resume of extra-curricular activities, frequently think scholarships and merit based aid are impossible to obtain. This may be a costly mistake.

What does make a student attractive to many colleges? **Admission officers (AO)** are not necessarily seeking the one-dimensional student: the one that has excellent grades and nothing else to show for after four years in high school. An **AO** likes to see a student who has participated in athletics, music, drama and art, student government, church, scouts, volunteerism and clubs. They are seeking the multi-dimensional individual. The **AO** is seeking the student who is a good student and who will become engaged in the university through involvement similar to that in high school.

One more point on building a resume. Internships or part-time jobs will be beneficial for the student to have on that college application. That is especially true if the internship or work was in a field that the teen plans on studying at the college. Such experience shows a desire and direction in life and **AOs** like that.

Grades are very important and so are those SAT and ACT test scores. What is more important however is to identify schools that place your pre-college teen in the top quartile of his/her incoming freshman class. Conversely, if your teen's GPA is 3.8 and the average incoming freshman student has a 3.9 then there is nothing special about your student's grades. You are far more likely to receive merit based aid from a school that views your teen as a good academic recruit. Couple this with a well rounded resume and you are putting yourself in a good position for free money.

It is important to find out the award history of the colleges being considered. This will allow you to better determine if there is a chance for aid and how much might be offered. The schools do not typically make this information available but a good internet sleuth will be able to find it easily. Since the data you receive will be from prior years and is not exact, it can only be used as a good gauge.

Private scholarships are offered by organizations, associations, businesses and groups other than the college itself. They are frequently misunderstood and therefore not taken advantage of fully. There are thousands of private scholarships based on academic success. Many have additional required criteria for students to be considered. The private scholarships are usually given in $500 and $1,000 increments and seldom reach the $5,000 level.

The key to a successful scholarship campaign is for your teen to approach it like working a part time job. He/she needs to apply for dozens of scholarships after thoroughly searching what scholarships are available. Start with the high school guidance counselor, local organizations and associations, businesses, and do not forget employers of Mom and Dad, aunts and uncles, and grandparents. Churches, teacher associations and fraternal organizations also offer scholarships. The more aggressively this is approached, the more likely that money will be received.

In summary, those with grades above a 3.0 GPA, good test scores and a well rounded resume should pursue scholarship opportunities both at the universities as well as through private sources. It will take work but with diligence and persistence it will pay financial rewards.

20

Collegiate Athletics
As an Investment

Anytime I find myself making comparisons to note how different things are today than when I was a youth, I am reminded that this sure is a sign that I am getting older! Fewer things are more worthy of this comparison than youth sports.

As a child growing up in the 70's, sports was an integral part of my life as well as for most of my friends: baseball in the spring, soccer or football in the fall, basketball or wrestling in the winter. There were no choices where we played and it was simple... we played in the local recreation league with all of our buddies and neighbors. Dads were the coaches and older siblings were the umpires and referees.

Summer was for playing in the yard, pick-up basketball games at the park, neighborhood baseball games with ghost runners, pitcher's hand out and of course, family vacations. Sports were simple. Life seemed less complicated.

Have things changed! Today, youth athletics is big business filled with year round sports, individual trainers, travel teams, professional uniforms, practice jerseys and, oh yes, high fees. By the ages of 9 and 10 many kids-are being forced to concentrate on a single sport or they risk the chance of falling behind or so we are led to believe.

My daughter Mary loves to play soccer. She plays on a select team that is coached and trained by professionals with no parental involvement. The fees are fifty times what my parents paid for me to play soccer when I was her age. She plays in the spring and the fall, and then plays indoor soccer in the winter and 3v3 soccer in the summer! (Just because I am writing the book doesn't mean I have not succumbed to the same pressures you have!)

I think the evolution of youth sports can be summarized in a conversation I had with Mary this past summer. We were on our way to one of her games about an hour from our house and in another state. I don't believe I played any sport that far from home until I was in high school! As we pulled up to the complex where the game was to be played, Mary sighed and said, "Oh no, we are playing on turf again!" My 10 year old had played enough times on artificial turf that she had formed an opinion that she would prefer to play on real grass!

Why are we spending hundreds and sometimes thousands of dollars for our kids to play youth sports? All too often and for too many families it is their wishful solution to the college cost dilemma: their college savings plan. If we spend the money today on proper training and coaching and select the right club teams, then we stand a good chance of our kids getting their college paid for through athletics. Have you noticed that most of the youth sports clubs even promote how many of their players went on to play in college?

Unfortunately this line of thinking about such "investments" for college might be very misguided. In this chapter I will explore the realities of scholarship opportunities at the various levels of college athletics.

The decisions that accompany the opportunities to play collegiate sports are complex. They certainly involve much more than our youngsters' athletic skills and abilities. Other critical factors need to go into the decision making process including a student's desire to play the sport at a highly competitively level; the student's academic strength; and of course, the value of the scholarship compared to the time required to participate.

The desire to play any particular sport at the college level has to be very strong and must match the student's skills and abilities. They must be willing to put in countless hours of practice time, often at the expense of social life opportunities. Students must accept that most of their time outside the classroom will be dedicated to their sport through practice, study tables, travel and early curfews. That may be more than some athletes are willing to commit to.

Certainly for those with special talents and abilities who will compete at the highest level of participation, such a decision still needs to be pondered. When all the factors are taken into consideration, the top athlete may be happier, less stressed and enjoy college more playing at a lower level of competition even if it is in an intramural program.

Those students who do achieve success at the varsity high school level are likely to have opportunities to play in college. That does not mean that every young man or woman who plays well in high school will ever be seen on television in college competition. In fact, most opportunities to play will come from small private or public colleges that you or your young adult may have never heard about previously.

The love of the game may not include the dream of playing on television or traveling first class across the country for the big competition. While a student may have had a rewarding and successful high school career in one or more sports, the love of the game may not include the high levels of competition and commitment required at the collegiate level. This issue alone demands some serious discussion before any decisions are finalized.

Just how good is our son or daughter in the chosen sport? An honest and more accurate assessment of the skills, abilities and talents is probably going to come from the high school or club coach. Parents, if we are honest, we realize that our objectivity is certainly clouded by our love for our kids. The coach or trainer can undoubtedly provide us with a more objective assessment from which we can then determine if the pursuit of an athletic scholarship or even participation at a collegiate level is realistic.

Once an accurate assessment is known and the decision to move forward with collegiate sports has been made, the pursuit of an appropriate school and program is underway. There are four levels of competitive college athletics. The NCAA (National Collegiate Athletic Association) is subdivided into three divisions based on the level of competition: DI, DII and DIII. The NAIA (National Association of Intercollegiate Athletics) is not affiliated with the NCAA and its membership includes over a couple hundred small universities and colleges.

NCAA Division I is big business: a multi-billion dollar industry. These colleges and universities will often recruit nation-wide for the athletes who will help their teams win and subsequently put more spectators in the stadiums. Athletes are recruited to help drive school revenue and at this level, players have a "job." That job is to work for their sport and the college that owns them. This may or may not be a desirable position for your son or daughter.

NCAA Division I sports is the pinnacle of college sports and it is rare to find a player possessing the skills to play at this level. In fact according to the NCAA website only 2 to 3% of high school athletes go on to play Division I sports. If your son or daughter is blessed to have the skills to play at the Division I level chances are you are already aware of that so what about the scholarships?

Many people think that at the DI level all students are on full ride scholarships. Sadly, this is not true. In fact, only four sports will generally offer "full rides."

Those are men's and women's basketball, men's football and women's volleyball. The NCAA limits the total money colleges can offer in scholarships; coaches frequently split the scholarships into partial awards to spread the offers to more players.

While still a very competitive level of sports, Division II athletics places more emphasis on the student athlete than the revenue an athlete generates. DII athletes also have the ability to earn scholarships based solely on their athletic ability, however full scholarships are highly unlikely. A well rounded student with good grades and test scores is much more likely to receive greater financial assistance than the student who can only offer their on-the-field abilities.

Both Division I and II athletes must pass through the NCAA Initial-Eligibility Clearinghouse, the organization that determines a student's eligibility. There are very specific requirements that must be followed and met in order for a student to be able to play DI or DII sports. It is recommended that this eligibility clearance be accomplished in the junior year of high school.

Division III student athletes are students first and athletes second. DIII schools are unable to offer scholarships based exclusively on athletic ability. Any offer will be based on grades, test scores and overall application information which may include athletic abilities. Recruiting is limited. In many cases the student athlete will need to promote him or herself to the school. Since athletic scholarships are not offered, a student planning to play at a DIII school does not have to register with the NCAA Clearinghouse. Almost 40% of NCAA college athletes play at the DIII level.

The National Association of Intercollegiate Athletics (NCIA) is not affiliated with the NCAA. It is a group of approximately 280 smaller universities and colleges that do offer athletic scholarships. Although there are few recruiting rules in the NCIA, there are strict academic requirements.

Regardless of the level, Title IX has provided greater opportunities for young ladies in collegiate athletics. Many schools struggle to find enough females to fill their rosters. Opportunities do exist if female athletes are willing to attend certain schools.

The overwhelming majority of students who play collegiate athletics will never earn a living playing a sport. In other words they are a *student-athlete* with an emphasis on *student.* Their focus should be on plans to become productive members of society and of the work force after college.

Career choice must be considered if the desired or preferred avenue to college is through athletic scholarships. As they select a career a review of the demands for that particular major should be taken into consideration. Time demands for certain majors can be enormous. For example, a degree that involves a lot of science classes will more than likely require a significant amount of lab time over and above class time. A student interested in pre-med or pre-law, whose undergraduate degree plays a significant role in admittance to these advanced programs, may find it wise to focus solely on the academics.

Often, good athletes who decide to pursue playing sports in college will need to develop a self-marketing program. Your young athlete must drive this process even if you consider hiring assistance. College coaches, just like admissions officers, want to know that the student has been significantly engaged in the process.

Unless your son or daughter is an elite athlete recruiters will not likely make the first contact. Your son or daughter will need to reach out to the schools of interest. E-mails, letters, phone calls, and videos will all likely be necessary to gain the attention of a college coach.

Some families will hire a consultant to help with this process. There are companies that will do everything from contacting schools on your child's behalf to creating marketing videos of your athlete. Fees range from a couple of hundred dollars to a few thousand dollars. Before hiring a firm, ask for references and talk with families who have used it, and speak with your child's coach about his/her experience with the firm. Make sure you understand what the company will do for you and what you or your athlete will be responsible for doing.

If you son or daughter ventures down the road of college athletics the single greatest factor in the school selection should be the academic compatibility of the school to the student. Selecting the right school for the sport with little regard to the academic fit is very often a recipe for failure. Always remember *student* comes first in *student* athlete.

21

Scenarios

I have shared with you a number of ideas your family should consider when selecting and paying for college for your teen. The following scenarios are presented in a before and after format so you can see the impact of our planning components on the outcomes.

Scenario #1

Mr. and Mrs. "We Won't Qualify." Probably one of the more common scenarios we run across is the family that is certain that they do not stand any chance for financial aid. In reality the family's ability to qualify may be much greater than the parents think.

This family has one child, a high school junior, who is a very good student and is looking to go to a more expensive and prestigious school. Mom and Dad have done a commendable job with their own finances. In fact, they own a $145,000 home that is paid off, and have no other debts with savings and investments of $394,000. Additionally they have an income of $88,000 per year so it is easy to see why they might believe that their chances of qualifying for any aid would be minimal.

They are right that their **EFC** is rather high, in fact it is $24,000 a year. That alone would eliminate their opportunity for aid from many schools, but their son is looking at four schools, each with an annual average cost of attendance of $40,000. Based on this alone, they are a **Category II Family,** which means they will qualify for some amount of financial aid. Without any adjustments to their financial picture they have a need of $16,000 ($40,000 **COA** less $24,000 **EFC**). Failure to complete the **FAFSA** would have caused this family to miss out on $64,000 ($16,000 x four years) of aid opportunity. Had even 50% of that come in the form of **gift aid** that would have been a loss of $32,000 in free money.

Since they are a **Category II Family** a closer inspection of their finances is required to see if there is an aid optimization opportunity. Some of their investment accounts earmarked for retirement were found not to be in retirement accounts, therefore those investments were counting against them in the **EFC** calculation. Those funds were moved into an account that did not count in the **EFC** calculation and their **EFC** was reduced from $24,000 to $17,000. That meant another $28,000 of aid opportunity over the four years of school. Failure to complete the **FAFSA** form for this family would have resulted in a lost aid opportunity of $92,000!

As a result of these changes the parents needed to now look closely at the aid award history offered by the four schools that their son was considering. This would not have been a concern had they been a **Category III family** with no financial aid opportunities. With the **COA** of $40,000 minus the revised **EFC** of $17,000 the **NEED** is now $23,000 per year.

We looked at the four schools. Two met 50% of the **NEED** while the other two met 100% of the family's **NEED**.

Focusing then on those 100% schools, both offered 50% of the **NEED** in gift aid ($11,500 per year). Selecting either of these schools over the other two resulted in a $46,000 savings for a family that contemplated not completing the **FAFSA** at all!

The school they selected happened to be only forty-five minutes from their home. A local community college offered the basic education classes for this school at a fraction of the price. In fact, if the student had chosen this option he would have used the same text books and have had some of the same teachers from that four-year institution. The community college option would have saved the family about $30,000 over two years and the student would have had a seamless transition to the four-year institution with no adverse academic problems.

Scenario #2 Mr. & Mrs. "We R. Strapped" is a family with whom far too many other families can relate. This is a family in an affluent neighborhood with three youngsters in private schools, a nice house, significant income, yet they are drowning in debt. This family is not financially reckless. They are uninformed about how to accomplish the daunting task of life today, college for three children in a few short years and retirement approaching faster than ever imagined.

They have a home worth $400,000, a 15-year mortgage of $200,000, credit card debts of $16,000, a 401k loan of $25,000 and two car loans totaling $31,000. They have an income of $160,000, and savings and investments for college of $90,000. They are not too concerned about retirement because of a substantial pension through an employer.

This family was sure that financial aid would be a certainty given the amount of debt they had amassed over the last few years. However upon an initial review of their **EFC** they were shocked to find that it was $36,000 per year. An analysis of their situation identified that their college savings was having a significant impact on the **EFC** due to the fact that it was all titled in the children's names. Additionally there was no positive impact from the extensive installment loan payments because the **Federal Methodology (FM)** does not take debt into consideration.

Also the parents were attempting to be mortgage free by the time they retired so they were aggressively paying down the15-year mortgage. Given all of their other expenses this mortgage was harming their finances more than helping. Their credit card debt, the 401k loan, and the car payments were resulting in over $1,500 per month of <u>high interest</u>, yet <u>non-deductible</u> debt for this family.

Consolidating their non-mortgage debt into a new 30-year mortgage with an increase in interest rate of .5% (1/2%) they have an additional monthly savings of $1,626 ($19,512 annually). Their additional tax deductible interest will result in tax savings of $5,400 for a total increase in cash flow of $24,912 each year.

This dramatic increase in cash flow will greatly help them pay for college but now it was time to see if anything could be done with their **EFC** of $36,000. Remember that many of their college assets were titled in their children's names thus having a negative impact on the **EFC**. After consultation with their CPA, a re-titling of their investment accounts removed said assets from the children's calculation thus reducing their **EFC** to $21,000 per year.

With college beginning next year for their oldest of three, this family is now in a position to afford their **EFC** of $21,000 per year given that they just improved their annual cash flow by almost $25,000. Proper selection of a college for each student coupled with the use of the **Stafford Loans** would allow them to navigate their way through the college years without any problem.

Once the college years were completed they would redirect the improved cash flow toward paying off the house. This strategy coupled with a mortgage acceleration program would still have them mortgage free in fifteen years. That was their plan all along, even though the path they were going down was not likely to lead to that dream.

Scenario #3   Mr. and Mrs. "Overlap" are an interesting family. They were planning and forecasting for all college years ahead of time and it paid off for them. For simplicity's sake, let us assume that Mr. and Mrs. "O" have the same financial picture as Mr. and Mrs. "We Won't Qualify" in scenario #1: the $145,000 home is paid off and they have $394,000 of savings and investments with an income of $88,000. Obviously their initial **EFC** would then be the same $24,000 per year.

Let us however change the family dynamics and college selection. The O's have three children: a senior, a sophomore and an 8th grader. The senior is looking at schools ranging from $20,000 per year to $25,000 per year. Given their **EFC** of $24,000 there does not appear to be any financial aid opportunity. Or is there?

Over the next eight years it is quite likely (assuming all stay in college for at least four years) they will have four of the eight college years with two students in school at the same time.

When multiple students are in college at the same time the **EFC** gets split almost in half. So each student in this case would have an **EFC** of just over $12,000 per year when two are in college. With that change, the oldest child will qualify for financial aid in her junior and senior year. The family reviewed the financial award history of the schools under consideration and selected the college with the highest gift aid. Although they knew they would not be eligible for financial aid in their daughter's freshman and sophomore years, I recommended they complete the FAFSA so they could qualify for Stafford Loans in those first two years.

<u>Scenario #4</u>   Single "Mom or Dad" is another common situation that is frequently encountered. In this situation, Mom has three children and is planning to send them to college. She has an income (including child support) of $41,000, savings of $6,000, a stock investment of $17,000, a mutual fund of $20,000, a brokerage account with additional mutual funds of $89,000, and an IRA of $29,000. The Dad is not participating in paying for college. Since the girls spend more than half of their time with Mom, it is her financial information that goes on the **FAFSA**.

Single Mom would like to help each child as much as she can but she realizes that her relatively low income is not going to permit her to save much for retirement. Therefore most of her assets needed to be preserved for her own financial future. She had told the teens she is sure that they will qualify for financial aid.

She was quite surprised to find that her **EFC** was $18,000 per year. In fact she was more than surprised! She was very anxious because this meant she was going to be faced with spending most of her assets to pay for college thus jeopardizing her chances of a retirement, or she was going to saddle each of her children with a large amount of student loans. Neither was a scenario she desired.

Upon review of her financial situation it was determined that the assets she had earmarked for retirement were in accounts that were really escalating her **EFC**. We eliminated some of the types of investment funds and replaced them with financial instruments that did not figure in the aid process which simplified her taxes and resulted in a dramatic reduction of the **EFC**.

We moved her money into a balance of IRAs, variable annuities and permanent life insurance, all of which have no annual tax consequence. Most importantly, the changes allowed her to file the **1040A** . Filing a **1040A** or **1040EZ** gives their family an automatic zero **EFC**.

We gave her sufficient access to cash from the life insurance while sheltering the balance of the investments she intended all along to use for retirement in annuities and IRAs.

With **EFC** eliminated, the only major concern remaining was to help her children select schools that met a high percentage of need since their only expense would be the **gap** or the need not met. For example a $30,000 per year school meeting 75% of the NEED leaves Mom and student responsible for $7,500 per year easily managed through Stafford Loans, part-time work and limited contributions from Mom. She was able to protect her financial future without saddling the future of her children with large student loans.

The chart that follows shows very clearly the impact of an **EFC** of **zero.**

COA	$ 30,000
EFC	$ 0
NEED	$ 30,000
NEED MET (75%)	$ 22,500
GAP (family out of pocket)	$ 7,500

Scenario # 5 Mr. and Mrs. "Entrepreneur" are an unfortunate reality of today's economic climate. Life has been rolling along without any problems and hardly a care in the world. Over the last few years income has been in excess of $180,000 per year. Savings and investments have been mostly put back into the family business. College and retirement were not a concern because the incomes that Mom and Dad both drew from their family-owned retail business were significant. It had always been planned that they would pay for about half of college for their two girls, a junior and seventh grader, out of income with the other half coming from $150,000 in a stock mutual fund. They figured that college was going to cost them about $30,000 per year.

Recently their business was impacted by economic circumstances outside of their control. Their collective incomes went from $180,000 to about $90,000 and they had to take out a line of credit on the business in order to keep it afloat. The outlook for the foreseeable future was not good. To make matters worse, their college mutual fund account was now worth about $75,000 or half of what is was only a few months prior.

Mr. and Mrs. "E" were perplexed as to what to do. They desperately wanted to allow their older daughter to attend the school of her choice however the cost was going to be slightly over $30,000 per year. While they had filled out the **FAFSA** form in January, it was based on their income from the previous year when they knew there was no way they would qualify for aid. They also knew that it was not going to be possible for them to afford college from their income like they had planned.

I was able to present them with a couple of options that would keep their daughters' dreams alive without further harming the parents' own finances. The first option was to have the older daughter contact the chosen school and explain in detail the changes in the family's economic position to enable the institution to use professional judgment and offer a financial aid package that considered the family's new financial situation.

The second option was for their daughter to attend a local community college that had a reciprocal agreement with the preferred school. For less than $8,000 per year the daughter could take her first two years of classes at the community college and then transfer to the four-year school for her last two years. This would allow the family to reduce their costs by almost 40%. It would also buy them some time for the opportunity for the business to get back on its feet.

While the college did come back with a much improved financial aid package, the family chose the second option of community college. They planned to revisit the decision at the end of the freshman year.

Scenario #6   Mr. & Mrs. "I Pay Tax" own a successful business with income over $300,000 per year. They also have substantial assets that would be included in the financial aid calculation. They have only one child, a junior, and absolutely no hope of qualifying for financial aid, which makes them a Category Three family.

In these cases, we employ tax strategies to help the family fund college education for their children in a tax-advantaged way. This kind of college planning will not reduce immediate out-of pocket cost, but rather will increase family funds available for *future* college costs by reducing taxation. In other words, every dollar saved on taxes is a dollar in your pocket that can then be put towards future college costs.

After consulting my in-house tax professional, I recommended that Mr. & Mrs. IPT hire their son as an employee and put him on their business payroll. The purpose of this strategy is to shift income to the student, who is likely in a much lower tax bracket. All payroll expenses (wages, taxes and fees) are deductible by the business, and therefore reduce business income, which reduces Mom and Dad's taxes. The student then claims these wages on his tax return, and pays taxes on them at a much lower tax rate than Mom and Dad. Also, the student can then qualify for education tax benefits that the parents are phased out of due to their high income level.

By paying their student a $20,000 salary, Mr. & Mrs. IPT increased their business deductions by $21,766 ($20,000 wages and $1,766 payroll taxes), which reduced their income taxes by $7,618, resulting in a net tax savings of $5,852 ($7,618 income tax savings less $1,766 payroll tax increase) per year.

The student then files his own tax return and reports the $20,000 wage income. Since the student is now providing more than half of his own support with earned income, he can claim his own personal exemption and he gets the standard deduction for a single tax payer. The American Opportunity Credit reduces all resulting taxes to zero, AND the student qualified for the refundable portion of this credit, resulting in a $1,000 refund on his tax return.

All together, this family generated a "tax scholarship" of $6,852 per year ($5,852 tax savings for parents plus $1,000 tax refund for student), which will result in savings of $27,408 over a four year period! In addition, this strategy opens up the window for some asset gifting strategies which will result in even further tax savings!

Although there is great opportunity here, you should absolutely consult a tax professional before implementing such a strategy since every situation is different. You will need to know the IRS rules that govern the employment of family members and whether or not favorable payroll tax rules apply. In addition, you will want to be clear on whether or not the Kiddie Tax rules apply, what the annual gift exclusions are, and whether the parents or the student claims the student's personal exemption.

Although these are some of the more common scenarios I have seen in my many years of college planning, almost every family I meet with has a slightly different circumstance that makes their situation unique. In every scenario, thousands of dollars were ultimately saved. In my opinion, it is an almost certainty that a family who fails to develop a plan to pay for college will leave thousands or even tens of thousands of dollars on the table.

Whether or not your situation resembles one of these case studies, I hope that you have gleaned from this section the utmost importance of planning ahead.

22

Putting it All Together

It is my sincerest hope that by this point in the book I have imparted to you valuable and usable information in the college and retirement process. Furthermore I hope that I have motivated you to take action to develop your family's plan. I assure you that planning will most certainly reap rewards for you and your college bound children.

Step one is to recognize where you are in the process. How much time do you have before your child goes to college? How much planning have you already done? How much more do you need to learn? These are questions that you need to answer.

Step two is to conduct a family meeting including Mom and Dad and the teens who are college bound in the near future. This should be a high level meeting with an agenda that discusses goals, aspirations, concerns, and timelines. It should be an exciting meeting with the premise that the family wants to develop a plan that is going to get the best education for the student without harming your retirement.

Obviously, input and buy-in from your teen(s) is critical because half of this plan (the college part!) is about him or her. Helping the emerging adult understand the financial impact of paying for school is an important component in getting him/her to actively participate in the process.

The next step is to begin identifying your "paying for college" team members. Quite possibly you already have relationships with some of the people we have discussed. Go to them and share your preliminary plan with them. Ask them for referrals to the other people who you need to complete your team. More often than not, these individuals work regularly with other people in the college planning arena and can introduce you to qualified professionals who you can talk to.

I find the reverse calendar to be very effective in planning long term and I use it in many aspects of my business and personal life. I encourage you to do the same for the college timeline. Simply start with the end event or goal in mind and work backwards to establish time frames and deadlines that cannot be missed.

I also encourage you to have your team members participate in helping you complete this calendar. Once established, a regular "family meeting" time should be determined. In each session you identify upcoming events and deadlines as well as assign responsibility for the particular task. As a note, the time and frequency of this meeting should be such that you have no distractions and ample time to discuss the items at hand. A rushed meeting with constant distractions will invariably result in an unsuccessful meeting.

A note on assigning of tasks: by all means your teen should play an integral role in this process. In fact I have stated in previous chapters that communications with the colleges should always be done by the student. There are, however, aspects of this process that are better suited for Mom or Dad to complete. As tasks are assigned, each family member should have his/her proportional share of work to complete prior to the next meeting.

Do not underestimate the power of this scheduled time together to discuss your plan. Also do not be tempted to take such meetings lightly or treat them as anything other than a family business meeting. After all, you are talking about a plan that is going to cost many thousands of dollars.

It is my promise to you that when you send your child off to college or whatever it is that he/she chooses to do after high school, you will do so with the knowledge that you have done everything possible to put both you and your son or daughter in the best position for success while protecting your own financial future.

23

Life's Lessons

I know that the focus of this book is on the financial aspects of paying for college however, I cannot help but spend at least one chapter talking about the valuable lessons that can be achieved through this process.

Financial planning has been my profession since leaving college. For the past 20 years I have sat with thousands of families and have discussed their finances. If I have heard it once I have heard it a thousand times, *"I wish I would have learned this at a younger age."* Managing money is NOT something that is commonly taught in grade school, high school or even college (unless it happens to be your major!) and yet we all need to know how to do so.

You can start these lessons today with your kids. Involve them in the financial aspects of paying for college. They need to know about the loans, the interest, the payments, the time-value of money, the income that they can earn from a particular job, the cost of an apartment, the cost of owning a car, the cost of personal and property taxes, what utilities cost and much more. One of the key components of sending a child to college is to prepare him/her for the future. These things are in the teen's immediate future and the lessons should start well before college begins.

Parenting is without question the most rewarding and challenging task in life that I have come across in my 43 years on this Earth. I spend many nights wondering if I am providing my young children with all they need to be happy and to have successful lives. I can only imagine how my desire for those things for my kids will be exponentially increased as each of them graduates from high school and contemplates the next wonderful stage of life.

I encourage you as I have many others to have a talk with each of your children about happiness and success. It is too easy to become immersed in the academics and the finances concerning college and lose sight of the fact that this is a time for them to grow and to learn about how to be independent. They will exercise their minds and consider multiple directions. For the first time, they get to choose.

Don't be alarmed, I am still the finance guy that has written this book, and believe it or not, happiness does play into this *paying for college process*. How many people do you know in their 30's, 40's and 50's who are unhappy doing what they do and wish they could go back in time? Dare your children to dream and ask them to imagine. Challenge them on their thoughts only to test the depth of those dreams and not to stomp on them. Guide them in this journey so that they can see their dreams through the eyes of someone with a little more life experience. Success and happiness, could we ask anything more from a college experience?

Develop a plan. Work it with your team members. Set goals, have regular meetings, and consult with experts. These are all phrases that I have used throughout the course of this book. This process, in my opinion, is a critical part of having success in any major personal or business endeavor you may choose to take on.

What a great way of teaching by example to your children. At some point in the future, beyond graduation from college, they will look back and recognize that Mom and Dad approached major challenges in life with careful planning. They took the time to make educated and informed decisions. Is this not what we hope that they do as they venture out on their own?

I often think about my own children as parents and I wonder what they will say about Grandpa to their kids. My hope is they will say that he was a good man who valued excellence, strove to be a better person, had a passion to help others and truly believed the only thing limiting us was in our own minds.

We live in a great country with wonderful opportunities, rich with success stories from generations past. However, we are going through one of our most challenging economic times we have seen in almost 90 years. People have lost jobs, families have lost their homes and many are questioning opportunities for next generations. Thoughts and words are so powerful that I believe we must remain positive even in the midst of turmoil.

Do your kids a favor and let them know that in spite of everything they may hear, in spite of what they may see on the news, and regardless of what they may read, their dreams can and will come true. They are destined to achieve everything they want in life but first they must believe they can. What better gift can you give to them and to yourself than a belief and vision of happiness and success?

I wish you well.

Sincerely,

Scott T. Moffitt

Glossary

ACADEMIC YEAR - The school (academic) year is usually nine months (fall and spring semesters), but the period may vary according to the school and program.

ACG - Academic Competitiveness Grants, started in 2006, are for Pell Grant recipients in the first or second year in college.

ADJUSTED GROSS INCOME (AGI) - AGI is a line on the IRS form indicating federally taxed income after adjustments have been made.

ADVANCED PLACEMENT (AP) - Many high schools offer AP classes that enable students to go on to higher level courses in college. Some colleges may award credit if students earn high grades in AP exams.

ALLOWANCES - These amounts are allowed as deductions by college financial aid formulas. They include: Tax Allowance, Income Protection Allowance, Employment Expense Allowance, and Asset Protection Allowance.

AMERICAN OPPORTUNITY CREDIT (AOC) - This is an education tax credit that is 40% refundable. Maximum credit is $2500 per student per year for the first 4 years of undergraduate work. Only qualified educational expenses apply. Consult a tax professional for further details.

ASSETS - Assets are property, including cash, savings and checking accounts, investments, trust funds, money market funds, mutual funds, CDs, stocks, bonds, real estate, business assets, and mortgages or loans owed to you. A few private colleges ask about the value of your cars and retirement accounts.

AVAILABLE INCOME - Aid formulas determine an income amount they consider "available" for use in calculating the Expected Contribution. Total income from all sources minus allowances is "available income."

AWARD YEAR - Period for which aid is requested; usually the academic year between July 1 of one year and June 30 of the following year.

BASE YEAR – Is the calendar year before the academic year for which aid is requested. The first base year for students entering as freshmen in the year 2009 began on January 1, 2008. Income data from each base year is used to calculate the Expected Family Contribution.

BUSINESS/FARM SUPPLEMENT - Private colleges that use the PROFILE aid application system require this form to collect additional information about business and/or farm assets.

CAMPUS-BASED PROGRAMS - The federal aid programs that are administered by the colleges are the Federal Perkins Loan, the Federal Supplemental Educational Opportunity Grant (SEOG), and Federal Work-Study.

CAPITAL GAIN - Income earned from the sale of an asset is a capital gain to be reported on tax returns.

CAPITAL LOSS - A loss resulting from the sale of an asset is a capital loss to be reported on tax returns.

COLLEGE COST NAVIGATOR - This is a software program available for purchase that will provide families extensive data and point by point comparisons for over 2,000 colleges nationwide. www.collegecostnavigator.com

COLLEGE SAVINGS PLANS - Under IRS Code Section 529 many states have contracted with an investment firm or mutual fund company to establish, run, and market education savings programs. Most plans encourage out-of-state residents to participate.

NOTE: At the time of the writing of this book, 529 plans were considered to be parental assets for financial aid purposes. Consult a financial aid professional for current rulings.

COLLEGE SCHOLARSHIP SERVICE (CSS) -The College Board's College Scholarship Service administers the PROFILE needs analysis system used by many private colleges to award their own aid funds to supplement federal aid funds.

COMPONENTS OF AID PACKAGES -Financial aid includes grants and scholarships, loans, and work-study awards.

CONTRIBUTION -The number of dollars expected from a student and/or parents toward college expenses before aid is awarded is termed "contribution."

COST OF ATTENDANCE (COA) -Each college uses its own standard figure for Cost of Attendance when awarding aid. It includes tuition, fees, room and board, books and supplies, transportation, and an allowance for miscellaneous personal expenses.

DEPENDENT STUDENT -A student who does not qualify as an independent student is dependent. Parents' (as well as the student's) assets and income will be considered by aid formulas.

DIRECT LOANS - Federal Stafford and Federal PLUS loans fall in either the Direct or FFEL category. If your school participates in the William D. Ford Federal Direct Loan Program, funds are lent directly by the U.S. government. At schools that do not use the Direct Program, the loans are of the FFEL (Federal

Family Education Loan) type, made through banks, credit unions, and other private lenders.

EARLY DECISION - Some colleges allow students to apply early for an admission decision on condition that students must agree to attend if accepted and to withdraw applications at any other schools.

EDUCATION IRA - Now called a Coverdell Education Savings Account and greatly expanded, this was a trust account set up in the name of a beneficiary in order to save for education expenses.

ELIGIBILITY - The amount of aid for which you are "Eligible" is the same as the "Need" for aid that has been calculated by the aid formulas that analyzed the family's financial data. Different aid formulas may calculate different results. "Eligibility" ("Need") may be met in part or in full by an aid package. If the family does not receive the full amount of aid for which it is "Eligible," there is an aid gap.

ELIGIBILITY QUALIFICATIONS - To be eligible for most aid programs, a student must be a U.S. citizen or eligible non-citizen, have a high school diploma or equivalent, have a Social Security number, be enrolled as a regular student studying toward a degree in an eligible program, be registered with the Selective Service if required, make satisfactory academic progress, show financial "Need" (according to aid formula calculations), and sign a certification statement on the FAFSA form. Schools also need to meet "institutional" eligibility standards set by the Department of Education.

EQUITY - Equity is the value of ownership in property. Home equity is the current value of the family residence less any amounts owed on it.

EXEMPTIONS - When figuring taxable income, the IRS allows a special deduction based on the number of persons in a family.

EXPECTED FAMILY CONTRIBUTION (EFC) - The number of dollars the family (student, spouse if any, and parents of dependent students) is expected to pay toward college expenses. There are two ways EFC is computed--by Federal Methodology (FM) and by Institutional Methodology (IM). (If the family does not receive aid for the full amount of the difference between the official cost of the college and the EFC, there is an aid gap.)

FAFSA - The Free Application for Federal Student Aid is the application form for all federal student financial aid.

FEDERAL METHODOLOGY (FM) - FM is a set of needs analysis formulas used to compute the Expected Family Contribution. It is used when awarding federal aid to students at public and private colleges.

FFEL LOANS - Federal Stafford and Federal PLUS loans fall in either the FFEL or Direct category. FFEL (Federal Family Education Loan) loans are made through banks, credit unions, and other private lenders. (At schools that participate in the William D. Ford Federal Direct Loan Program, funds are lent directly by the U.S. government.)

FORBEARANCE -A temporary postponement or reduction of student loan payments for a specific period of time. Interest continues to accrue during forbearance.

FSEOG - The Federal Supplemental Educational Opportunity Grant is a campus-based federal program for undergraduates with the lowest Expected Family Contributions (highest financial need for aid). Colleges award the funds.

FULL TIME - In most cases, full time is at least 12 credit hours in a term or 24 clock hours per week.

GAP - When an aid package does not meet the full amount of the difference between the official cost of the college and the family's Expected Contribution (EFC), there is an aid gap. "Unmet Need" is another term for aid gap. Student and parent loans are available to cover EFC and any Gap.

GIFT AID - Grants or scholarships that do not need to be repaid are gift aid.

GRACE PERIOD - The time period during which a borrower is not required to make payments of principal or interest.

GRANT - Grants are aid that does not need to be repaid. Financial aid formulas will not count this as income available toward the Expected Family Contribution. To the extent that it goes toward direct education costs, it is tax-free.

HOME EQUITY - This is home value minus mortgage and other debts owed on the property. Home equity is not counted in the federal aid formulas, (FM) but is counted by the institutional formulas (IM).

HOME EQUITY LINE OF CREDIT - Home equity loans may be set up so that the borrower can withdraw funds as needed.

HOME EQUITY LOAN - The borrower's equity in the primary residence is the collateral for a home equity loan. Interest is tax deductible on loans of up to $100,000 if the taxpayer itemizes on his or her tax return.

INDEPENDENT STUDENT - Federal rules say that a student can be considered independent if at least one of the following applies: the student is at least 24 years old, is married, has legal dependents other than a spouse, is an orphan or ward of the court, is an active duty member or a veteran of the U.S. Armed Forces, is enrolled in a graduate or professional program, or is a member of the armed services currently serving on active duty for other than training purposes. Private colleges sometimes have additional requirements and may require a contribution from an independent student's parents.

INSTITUTIONAL METHODOLOGY (IM) - A set of needs analysis formulas used to compute the Expected Family Contribution for awarding private (institutional) funds to students at private (and some public) colleges.

IRA - Individual Retirement Account. Contributions to tax-deferred retirement accounts are allowed as deductions by the IRS, but they count as Untaxed Income for financial aid purposes.

LIFETIME LEARNING TAX CREDIT - This credit is a non-refundable tax credit for an unlimited number of years for both undergraduate and graduate programs and is limited to $2,000 per tax return per year.

LOANS - Loans, such as student Stafford Loans and student Perkins Loans, are included in aid packages. Parents may use non-aid PLUS Loans or alternative loans to pay for Parents' Contribution or any aid gap.

MEANS-TESTED - One of the qualifications that help determine eligibility for Simplified Needs asset treatment is for the parents or dependent student (or independent student and spouse) to have received, during the previous 12 month period, benefits from certain means-tested federal benefit programs in which eligibility for or amount of benefits are determined on the basis of income or resources. These include Supplemental Security Income (SSI), Food Stamps, School Lunches, TANF, and WIC.

MERIT AID - Merit aid is based on the characteristics of the student, rather than on financial need. The characteristics could be academic achievement, athletic ability, musical talent, place of origin, etc.

NEED - Aid administrators subtract the Expected Family Contribution from the college's Cost of Attendance to determine the "Need" ("Eligibility") for aid. "Need" may be met in part or in full by an aid package.

NEEDS ANALYSIS - Determination of a family's Expected Contribution and "Need" ("Eligibility") for aid by examination of financial data is known as "needs analysis."

NET WORTH - Net worth is the total of all assets minus any liabilities or debts against these assets.

OUTSIDE SCHOLARSHIPS - Scholarship money from private organizations originates from "outside" the aid package. All or part of "outside" scholarships may be subtracted from already-awarded college grants and loans, because the total of family contribution and aid cannot be higher than the Cost of Attendance.

PACKAGING – Is the process by which an aid administrator puts together grant, scholarship, loan, and job components to build an aid package for a student.

PARENTS' CONTRIBUTION - The amount that aid formulas calculate parents must pay from their income and assets toward a dependent student's college costs before aid is awarded. It is added to the Student Contribution. The total of the two is called Expected Family Contribution.

PELL GRANT - A federal grant (as calculated by analysis of the FAFSA form) to undergraduate students with the greatest financial need.

PERKINS LOAN - A federal loan program with a low interest rate for students with high need. The Perkins Loan is a campus-based program.

PERSONAL ASSETS - Such assets include cash, savings and checking accounts, investments including trust funds, money market funds, mutual funds, CDs, stocks, bonds, real estate, and mortgages or loans owed. Aid formulas used by colleges that award private funds (IM) count the primary residence as a personal asset.

PLUS LOAN - PLUS is a federal loan program for parents of undergraduates. PLUS loans are not based on financial need. They depend on the parents' credit

and can be used toward the Expected Family
Contribution or to cover an aid gap.

PREFERENTIAL PACKAGING - Some colleges try
to attract certain students by offering them aid
packages that provide a mix with more grants and
fewer loans.

PROFESSIONAL JUDGMENT (PJ) - Aid
administrators have the ability to make decisions
based on special circumstances.

PROFILE - This is the College Scholarship Service's
institutional (IM) aid application and needs analysis
process, used by many private colleges.

RETIREMENT ACCOUNT CONTRIBUTIONS -
Contributions to an IRA, Keogh, SEP, 401k, 403b or
any other tax-deferred retirement accounts are allowed
as deductions by the IRS, but they all count as
Untaxed Income for financial aid purposes.

ROTC - Reserve Officer Training Corps programs are
available at many colleges. Options include: a
traditional four-year program that pays a small
monthly stipend during junior and senior years and
requires a service commitment and a competitive
ROTC scholarship program that covers a substantial
portion of costs in exchange for a longer service
commitment as an officer after college.

SATISFACTORY ACADEMIC PROGRESS (SAP)
- Aid rules require academic standards to be met in order for a student to continue receiving financial aid.

SCHOLARSHIPS - Financial aid that does not need to be repaid. They come in several varieties. Colleges may award private grant money as a named scholarship. It may be part of a need-based aid package, or it may be based purely on merit. Money from scholarships that are not connected with the college is considered as "outside" scholarships. Outside scholarships may benefit the college rather than the student if they would make the total of Family Contribution and already-awarded aid exceed the college's standard Cost of Attendance.

SELF-HELP - In addition to the Student Contribution, students also help pay for part of their college costs through student loans and work-study jobs, as designated in their aid packages.

SIMPLIFIED NEEDS TEST (SNT) - Federal Methodology will not count parents' or student's assets when calculating Expected Family Contribution if AGI of parents of a dependent student (or of independent student and spouse, if any) is under $50,000 and *EITHER* parents (or independent student and spouse, if any) file, or *qualify* to file, IRS Form 1040A or 1040EZ or are not required to file a tax return *OR* the parents or student (or independent student and spouse, if any) received during the previous 12 month period benefits from certain

means-tested federal benefit programs in which eligibility for or amount of benefits are determined on the basis of income or resources. These include Supplemental Security Income (SSI), Food Stamps, School Lunches, TANF, and WIC.

SMART GRANTS - National SMART Grants are for third or fourth year college students majoring in math, science, technology, or a "critical" foreign language.

SPECIAL CIRCUMSTANCES - Aid administrators may use Professional Judgment to take unusual situations into account when awarding aid.

STAFFORD LOANS - A federal loan entitlement program available to students who file the FAFSA form. When the student qualifies on a financial need basis, the loans are subsidized--the government pays interest on the loan while the student attends at least half time and for six months thereafter.

STUDENT AID REPORT (SAR) - SAR is a report generated by the federal aid application form (FAFSA). It shows whether the student qualifies for a Pell Grant and the amount of the FM Expected Family Contribution.

STUDENT CONTRIBUTION - The amount of college costs that aid formulas determine a student must pay before aid is awarded. If the student is dependent, it is added to the Parents' Contribution and the total is called Expected Family Contribution.

SUPPLEMENTAL EDUCATIONAL OPPORTUNITY GRANT (SEOG) - SEOG is a campus-based federal program for undergraduates with the lowest Expected Family Contributions (highest need for aid).

TITLE IV - Designates federal student financial aid programs authorized by the Higher Education Act. Programs include Pell Grants, SEOGs, Perkins loans, Stafford Loans, PLUS loans, and Federal Work-Study.

UGMA / UTMA - The Uniform Gifts to Minors Act (UGMA) in some states and the Uniform Transfers to Minors Act (UTMA) in other states allow setting up an account for the benefit of a minor (age varies according to state) as an irrevocable gift. A custodian manages the account. This type of account is counted by financial aid formulas as a student asset.

UNMET NEED -When an aid package does not meet the full amount of the student's calculated need for aid, there is "Unmet Need." Another term for "Unmet Need" is "aid gap."

UNTAXED INCOME - Most untaxed income and benefit items are counted by federal and institutional aid formulas. These include Social Security benefits, pensions, payments into retirement plans, tax exempt interest, child support received, welfare benefits, earned income credit, and living allowances. Private colleges also count depreciation and losses on businesses and real estate.

VERIFICATION - Verification means close inspection of all tax returns and other submitted financial documents to confirm that the amount of aid awarded is accurate. The federal government requires schools to verify approximately one-third of all aid forms submitted, but many colleges verify all applications.

WORK-STUDY - Federal Work-Study (FWS) is a federally-supported program of part-time employment based on an applicant's financial need. FWS allows qualified students to earn money to pay part of their college expenses. These earnings are taxable, but they are not counted by aid formulas.